PUNCHED, KICKED, SPAT ON AND SOMETIMES THANKED

PUNCHED, KICKED, SPAT ON AND SOMETIMES THANKED

MEMOIRS OF A CLEVELAND TV NEWS REPORTER

PAUL ORLOUSKY

Gray & Company, Publishers
Cleveland

Gray & Company, Publishers
www.grayco.com

ISBN 978-1-59851-114-7
Printed in the United States of America
1

CONTENTS

INTRODUCTION

I WAS A TV NEWS reporter for almost fifty years, most of them in Cleveland, specializing in investigative reports. During that time I saw a lot of things. Historic events. Horrific crimes. Bizarre behavior. Heartwarming deeds. And sometimes just hilarious, silly stuff.

And a lot of people saw me—on their TV screens, often live, on some sidewalk somewhere, holding a microphone in someone's face trying to get an answer. Or standing out in the cold on the scene of breaking news, trying to tell viewers what was happening (in ninety seconds or less).

Now, I want to share stories about things I saw but viewers didn't. What went on behind the camera. What happened on the way to the scene in a tiny helicopter, or crouched inside a sweltering news van with my photographer on a stakeout. What I heard in a judge's office or a courtroom lobby after an eventful trial. The internal workings of a news operation that shaped the reporting you saw on screen. The threats I received from angry subjects of an investigation, such as shady business owners, politicians, and sometimes even cops . . .

My wife says I wrote this book because I love talking about myself. I know better than to argue with my wife. But over the years, I've been asked a lot of questions by viewers, over and over. "Why did you do *that* story?" "Weren't you scared to knock on that criminal's front door?" Even "Why is the weather always the first story on the news?" So I know viewers are interested in knowing more about the TV news business. And I'm a reporter, right? I'm compelled to tell stories and answer questions.

I mean for this book to be fun. My approach to life is simple: You can look at it either as a tragedy or a comedy. I chose comedy, in part because that was a way to get through many of the tragic situations I reported on and that people I encountered were forced to deal with. I don't mean to minimize their plights, but everyone in the crazy business of TV news needs a tool to keep their sanity, and humor was mine. (Who else gets to roll a bowling ball down the middle of a Cleveland city street as part of doing his job?)

Not every story is light-hearted, though. Reporting on the news brought me into contact with a lot of people's pain and sorrow. There is value in sharing some of those difficult stories, too.

If you've ever watched local TV news, I think you'll enjoy these back stories behind the news stories. I've kept them short and informative. Hopefully, you'll get a smile or a chuckle or two and also wind up a (slightly) better informed news consumer.

Many of my experiences were humorous, and some were painful, but most I found enlightening. I hope my reporting of the news over those fifty years helped viewers understand a bit more about what went on in our city. I hope I was able to make a difference for people. I wasn't always successful, but I always tried.

WHAT HAVE I GOTTEN MYSELF INTO?

"YOU OWE ME $240, AND if you don't pay, I'm gonna kick your ass!"

There I was, in a downtown Cleveland hotel room with two prostitutes and their pimp, and the pimp was angry. Very angry. He was a big guy and about twenty years younger than me.

What the heck have I gotten myself into?

It wasn't the first time I had wondered that. As an investigative reporter for TV news, such thoughts came with the job.

I found myself in dangerous situations sometimes. I didn't plan it that way, but it happens. You simply don't know how people will react to being challenged or questioned, or—in this case—being refused payment for their illegal services.

To be honest, I got an adrenaline rush from situations like this. Professionally, I lived for that rush. I couldn't wait to get back to the station to tell everyone what happened. I usually painted myself as the victim.

But not always an unwilling victim.

In this case, the hidden-camera investigation was my own idea. It didn't go exactly as planned.

It was, I admit, one of my dumber ideas: to show that the back pages of some weekly entertainment-oriented local newspapers were making prostitution easily available. (This was in the early 2000s, before such services migrated mostly to the internet.)

Let's prove it, I thought, and I pitched the idea. The news director would have to agree to renting hotel rooms for the investigation. He said OK.

Our 19 Action News was taking an aggressive approach to reporting at that time. This story certainly had sex appeal. Probably not much news value, since most everyone already knew what those back-page ads were for. But the station had asked me to come up with something sexy for the ratings—and what is sexier than sex?

We rented two adjoining hotel rooms. I was in one room with a couple of hidden cameras. Those were monitored in the adjoining room by two cameramen and our station security guard. They were ready to come out once I had made contact and the pimp had said enough to show this was a "sex for money" deal.

Clearly, we had no intention of paying for anything illegal. Yet that actually became the problem. A big one!

I had set up a code phrase for the guys in the other room. If things got at all rough after I said I was unwilling to pay, they were to rush into my room and rescue me. The code was "I don't think this is gonna work out."

With cameras rolling, I placed a couple of calls to phone numbers in the ads. I was wearing a wireless microphone with the transmitter in my pocket, and the wire and microphone running up my sleeve to my shirt cuff. After only about a half-hour I received a confirmation call back. Very shortly after that, there was a knock on the door. My three colleagues retreated into the other room.

I answered the door.

A huge guy stood there with two women. "You called?" he asked. I said yes and told them to come on in. They did. "Here's the deal," he said. "It's $160 for one of them or $240 for both."

I tried to get more information by acting dumb. (Some say that's my best trait.) I hemmed and hawed.

"What's it gonna be?" he said.

I hemmed and hawed some more. He was getting agitated.

"What's it gonna be?"

I then asked the most important question: "Are you a full-service agency?" That meant, in the terminology of the trade, sex for money. He answered that they were.

I now had what I needed to prove my story. And I now had to get out of the situation.

"You know, I don't think this is gonna work out," I said. The code phrase.

"What?"

"I don't think this is gonna work out," I repeated, expecting my troops to come to my rescue (and also grab additional video). They didn't. So I said yet again, "I don't think this is gonna work out."

"I don't care if this isn't gonna work out or not," the pimp said, pointing his finger in my face. "You owe me $240 for our time or we're gonna have a f***ing problem."

By now, I was getting nervous. I put the microphone in my sleeve right up to my mouth and said, loudly, "I DON'T THINK THIS IS GONNA WORK OUT." Still, nothing happened. I was in for a beating for sure.

Only one thing to do: I announced that I was a TV reporter and that all of this was being taped.

"Yeah, I thought I recognized him," one of the women said. Then they took off.

The video shows me looking back, directly at the hidden cameras, waving my arms wildly like a third-base coach telling a runner to run home, trying to signal the crew that they should get in there quickly.

By the time they finally came to my "rescue," the big guy and the women were already down the elevator.

From this event I learned two things. First, don't take chances with doing a dumb story that involves getting your ass kicked. Second, and more practical, check the batteries in the wireless. You guessed it; they were dead. The security guard and camera guys in the other room never heard me say the code phrase. After that, I carried extra batteries in my briefcase until the day I retired!

This wasn't the first time I found myself in a tough situation, and it wouldn't be the last. And yes, there were times when I did get roughed up. I just wasn't the kind of investigative reporter who liked do his investigating by sifting through government data and crunching numbers. Sure, stories about things like overtime abuse can be told that way, but it just wasn't my style. Plus, TV news relies on pictures, and the better way for us to do a story like that is to *show* someone doing something wrong. And that can lead to confrontation.

I became known in Cleveland for these kinds of news stories. It wasn't something I had planned, though. It just worked out that way. Actually, it's about the furthest thing from what I imagined a career in news would be when I got into it more than fifty years ago . . .

GETTING STARTED IN BROADCASTING

ELMIRA—MY HOMETOWN

TED BAXTER, THE CLUELESS ANCHORMAN on the old *Mary Tyler Moore Show*, used to boast about his humble beginnings, saying, "It all started out at a little 5,000-watt radio station in El Segundo . . ." I hope I was never that clueless guy, but I would have envied his beginnings. My start was at a tiny *500*-watt AM daytime station in Elmira Heights, New York.

A senior at my high school, Jessie Benson, got a job at a small radio station. Its call letters were WEHH, which stood for Elmira Heights, Horseheads—two suburbs of Elmira. I asked him about it and how he got the job. He told me he had to get an FCC license to be hired. This was because you had to know basic regulations and how to take transmitter meter readings for frequency deviation, plate current, and a few other things.

I talked my dad into taking me to the FCC office in Syracuse, New York, to take the test. He was a kind man, but being an engineer was very serious. During the one-hour drive he said, "Do you know this stuff?" I made the mistake of saying, "Well, if you fail you get a second chance." Bad move. "You don't think we're coming up here twice, do you?" he said. Long pause. I studied hard the rest of the way and passed.

Two months later, between my junior and senior year in high school, I saw Jessie on the street and asked what was going on at WEHH. He said that he was going to quit the next day because he had been drafted and was going to Vietnam. This was the summer of 1969. It was bold of me; but I asked if it was OK for me to go up to the radio station and apply for his job. "What do I care, I'm going to Vietnam," he said.

I went to the station. Frank Saia, the owner, had me read some wire copy that he tore from a United Press International teletype machine. It was on old-school yellow paper with blue ink. I read it. "Is Joe Orlousky your father?" he asked. I said yes. "You can start on Monday," he said. It turned out that he had gone to high school with my father and thought highly of him. It was probably the only reason I was hired. "But you start on the FM station until you learn the control board," Saia said. In those days no one listened to FM.

I started that Monday, Labor Day, September 1, 1969. After a couple of hours, a caller dialed in and thanked me for doing an all-oldies show. It was a country station and I didn't know much about country music. I had no idea I was playing all oldies. The next day, I had to cut my shift short because it was the first day of my senior year in high school.

The job was about as far away from my high school demeanor as possible. I was a happy guy, had good friends and had a blast in high school. However, when it came time to give a speech in English class, I'd try desperately to find a way to get out of it. I was shy speaking in front of people. Yet now, here I was a broadcaster. The difference was that at the radio station I was just a guy sitting in a room alone, talking, and spinning records. No one was looking.

Another station, WENY, was the kingpin in those days. In early 1970, I learned that their morning show had an opening and I applied for it. I was still a high school kid, but I think the general manager, Mike Steele, admired my chutzpah. He didn't hire me, though.

"Hey Ma, They Hired Me!"

Then, about a month later, Mike Steele called and offered me a weekend shift. I hung up and yelled, "Hey ma, Mike Steele just hired me at WENY!"

In the beginning, I played taped religious programs on Sunday morning. I could hardly wait until 11 a.m., when I got to do a music show until noon. Gradually, they gave me more time on the air, and I became the main guy covering for vacations.

About the second year I was at the station, news director Tom Seem came up to me and asked, "Why are you in college?" I didn't have a clear answer other than that is what my parents expected. "If you want to be a disc jockey, why don't you quit college and just do it?" he asked. "You need a lot of work because you're not very good."

I was stunned and kind of crushed. He was right, but it turned out he had an ulterior motive. "Listen, try news, cover City Council for me Monday night and see if you like it," he said. I did cover council, but I didn't like it—I loved it. Tom liked my copy, and the rest is history.

I got a small taste of the big time in the summer of 1973. I was working at the radio station and got off the air at 2 p.m. Some friends and I were heading up to Watkins Glen for the massive Summer Jam rock festival. As I was leaving, I told program director Steve Christy where I was going. "Hey, NBC Radio is looking for someone to do reports for them from the concert," he said. "You want these press passes?" Sure! He gave me a handful of passes and a phone number to use to call in reports.

It worked out great. The press area had a big tent, and we were at the base of the stage. The Grateful Dead, The Allman Brothers, and The Band performed. Crowd estimates topped 600,000. It was bigger than Woodstock. I phoned in to NBC three or four times. They used my reports, and a couple of weeks later sent me a check for $125. It was more than I made in a week at the radio station.

All through that last year of high school and college I worked in paid jobs at radio and TV stations. When time allowed, I worked at the college stations for free.

The Flood of '72

"It Sprinkled, It Rained, and It Poured"—that was the title of a record put out by some local talent during the days after waters from Hurricane Agnes forced rivers, including the Chemung River in Elmira, over their banks. Anyone who has worked or lived in Elmira can tell you about the "flood." It happened in June of 1972. Of all the people who lived through it, I may have had the most unique vantage point. Let me explain.

It didn't sprinkle too long, but it rained for days. We had been reporting on the rising waters of the Chemung. The night the flood happened, I had worked a long day at the radio station collecting whatever information I could. I left at about 6 p.m. and picked up my brother, Mike, from his job at a supermarket. It was pouring rain.

I went to bed about 10 p.m. The phone rang about 11 p.m. in my parents' room. My mother came into my room and said the station was calling. The DJ about to go on the air for the overnight show, Dave Allen, told me the police were predicting that the river was going to go over its banks, and he needed help in informing the public what streets were priority streets for evacuation.

I told my mom I was going to work. She was frustrated at how much time I spent there, much of it unpaid. She hadn't realized how hard I had been bitten by the "news bug." "Do you have to run down there every time they call you?" she asked. I said that the river was going to flood. "That river isn't going to flood," she responded. I said I had to go. Now my dad, who could sleep through almost anything, apparently got the gist. As I headed down the steps after getting dressed, I heard him say from their room, "If the river is gonna flood, you're not taking the car." I guess he was OK with my "news bug," but he made sense. I walked and hitchhiked down to the station.

The rest of the night was kind of a blur. I reported updates on the priority streets for evacuation on the radio. The priority levels were "get prepared," "get ready," then "leave." Then, I would go down from the seventh floor to the first floor and do the same on the TV station. I was in constant contact with the police department and would call every half-hour before going on the air. The list of priority streets grew quickly. Up and down I went every half-hour. When the "leave" order came from the police chief, it was for every priority that we had listed, even the ones that were told it was unlikely they would have to evacuate. That is when it became clear that this was serious!

I continued until 6 a.m., when legendary newsman and commentator Bernie Morley came in. The station was located in the Mark Twain Hotel, so I went down the hall and found a door unlocked and went to sleep for a couple of hours. Bernie was smart; he recorded a couple of newscasts and then got out of there!

When I woke up and looked out the window, there was muddy water everywhere. No electricity. I went back down the hall to the studio and saw the morning DJ, Jay "Jaybird" Flannery, general manager Mike Steele, and a couple of others. We knew we weren't going anywhere anytime soon. On the turntable was a half-played record that had been spinning when the power went out—Sammy Davis Jr.'s "Candyman." Maybe that was prophetic, because for the next couple of days all we had to eat was candy and snacks from the vending machines. Luckily in those days, vending machines weren't electric. You put your money in and pulled a lever. The bad part was that they didn't take anything but coins, and eventually we ran out of coins from petty cash.

During the days there, I was seven floors above a nightmare. I watched furniture bobbing inside the store across the street; eventually it broke out the windows and floated away. The same for the display cases at the jewelry store. More important was the view I had of the river.

The station had an old Bell and Howell wind-up 16mm camera that I had been using to film the devastation. Uprooted trees, garages, and even a couple of houses were coming down the river and crashing into the Walnut Street Bridge. At one point, I asked Mike Steele if we could get up on the roof for a better view. He made it happen. Just as we got there, a house hit the bridge, and one of the spans began swinging to the shore. I got the very end of it on film; a historic moment captured—partially, at least—for history.

Because the TV station was on the ground floor and was devastated by flooding, it was off the air for a long time. The film I shot didn't get processed until the fall, when I was back in college. I have never seen it.

An odd aside to this is that across the street from the station was another flooded business, a kind of hippie store, opened by two of my high-school classmates from Elmira Free Academy. It was called the People's Place. Those classmates were Larry Stemerman and Tommy Hilfiger. Yes, that Tommy Hilfiger. It is where he got his start as a high school senior. He certainly had a remarkable recovery from the flood!

When the water receded, we were able to get out of the building and survey the damage. What we saw from the seventh floor had been alarming, but what we observed on the ground was worse. Lives were ruined and many businesses never came back. I don't think I am going too far when I say that Elmira never completely recovered, despite some heroic efforts. The flood was just too much for what had been a declining industrial town to endure.

Since then, in Elmira, time has kind of been divided into "before the flood" and "after the flood." I will never forget the flood of '72. Not just for what I witnessed, but for what I witnessed afterward.

They Let Me on TV

WENY had a TV station as well as radio, and by the time I was a junior in college, they had me begin to report the news on TV. This went on until I graduated.

After graduating in 1974, I got a job at a different TV station in Elmira: WSYE TV, a Newhouse-owned station. I was hired at $95 a week to do just about anything they asked. I tried to sell commercials (poorly). I directed the news at times (poorly). I was the technical director in the control room who said, "Take camera one, camera two, roll film," and things like that. I had nothing to do with deciding what stories we covered. When they were short a reporter or anchor, I filled in. I did the on-air jobs the best; the off-air jobs were not my passion. But I needed a job, and I did whatever they asked.

Sometimes I would direct the first two segments of the news and then the weather, and then, during the one-minute commercial break after the weather, I would dash down the hall to the studio to read the sports on air. Carl Proper, the guy who did the weather, would dash in the opposite direction to replace me in the control room, where he would direct my sports segment. Somehow, we never collided as we rushed past each other in the hall.

BINGHAMTON—MOVING UP

The work I did for WSYE in Elmira was good enough to get me a job at a TV station in Binghamton, a larger market about sixty miles away. WICZ was owned by a TV tower manufacturer, Stainless Incorporated. The owner, Henry Guzewicz, had taken the station over because the previous owner owed him money for a new tower and couldn't pay for it. When Guzewicz took control, he changed the call letters to the last four letters of his family name, WICZ. At the time the place operated on a shoestring. The station was on the second floor above a tire store. Nonetheless, I was excited. I was moving up.

It's unlikely that any one day at a job will make you or break you. But in my case it did. It was my first night on the air as the 6 p.m. anchor at WICZ. And it was the first real tragedy I ever had to describe live on the air.

I arrived in Binghamton on a Sunday, a day before starting the new job in September 1975. That day, a couple of kids decided they would tempt the waters of a swollen Susquehanna River. They became stranded. Firefighters went out to rescue them, and one of the firefighters drowned. Monday morning when I got to work, I was told that just an hour earlier our chief cameraman, Nick Horsky, had videotaped a failed and fatal attempt to retrieve the fireman's body.

The fire chief, the assistant fire chief, and a motorman had been in a fire rescue boat that had capsized during the effort to recover their comrade. Nick videotaped the whole chilling scene. The chief and assistant chief died in raging waters. The video showed them clinging to the overturned boat, hanging on for dear life in what proved a futile effort against the angry current. Only the motorman survived. Later, a Sheriff's Department boat also capsized, but all on board survived.

That night I was on the air for the first time in a new market, telling this awful story. I said something like, "There is nothing I can say to describe what you are about to see; it speaks for itself. We already know the results." I let the video play and shut up.

It taught me a lesson. As an anchor or a reporter, you are not the story. The people in the events are the story. What more could I have said to add to the drama Nick had captured on his video? Sometimes you just have to know when to shut up.

I'll explain how this day changed my career in a moment.

On the Move Again

About ten months after I arrived at WICZ, I got a call from the news director at the market-leading station across town, WBNG TV. It was a powerhouse station. He wanted to talk to me about a job opening. I went and spoke to him. The first thing he brought up was that footage of the firemen drowning and how I handled it. That first day on the job at WICZ got me a new job and a pay raise.

At WBNG I hosted a live hour-long daily talk show and also anchored the midday news. The morning show was called, not surprisingly, *The Morning Show*. It was a gabfest about politics, community issues, and events. Occasionally, we'd get a big-name guest coming through town. A few stand out.

The Big Names

WBNG was a CBS affiliate and the sitcom *Alice* had premiered on the network a few weeks earlier. One of the stars was Vic Tayback, the actor who played Mel, the gruff owner of the diner where Alice worked. He was booked for my show. We did one segment talking about his new show and his career. He had been in some remarkable movies, *Papillon* and *Bullet* among them.

The next segment of my show was designed for him to be in character as Mel, doing a cooking segment. On *Alice* the previous week, a customer had died after eating Mel's signature chili. The death had nothing to do with the chili, but it made for a funny story line.

During the commercial, we moved to the cooking set and Vic put his apron and chef's hat on. He began by putting ground beef into the pan, then some beans and tomatoes. He stirred the stuff for a while then exclaimed, "Now for the secret ingredient." He reached over to a large pitcher of water and poured a lot of it into the pan. I said, "Why all the water?" He cupped his hand and gave me one of those slaps at the back of my neck that made a kind of pop sound. Very gentle but unexpected. He said, "Profit, ya dummy." He was in character and had set me up beautifully. Everyone had a good laugh. Including me.

The next big name to come through was Jerry Falwell. He wasn't very well known at the time. He was hosting a religious crusade the upcoming weekend at the Broome County Arena. Clearly, he was going on the show to ramp up attendance, and let's be honest: larger attendance equals larger contributions.

I believe he was on for two segments for about twelve minutes, total. The first segment was him talking about his recently formed Liberty University. It was followed by his pitch for the crusade. Next, he introduced a guy who played the piano and sang a hymn. We faded into a commercial break.

What happened next told me that this guy Jerry Falwell knew what he was doing. We came back from commercial and talked a bit more. He had his piano guy sing another hymn. At some point our floor director reached around the camera and gave me a two-minute warning. Falwell spotted it, stood up, and snapped his fingers at the guy singing on the other set, giving him the wrap sign.

The guy stopped within about three notes. Falwell had saved those last couple of minutes to pitch his crusade. I was left thinking, "I haven't heard the last of this guy." In a short time, everyone had heard of him.

We had a few musical guests. England Dan and John Ford Coley introduced their song "I'd Really Love to See You Tonight" on *The Morning Show*. It was memorable for me because my wife, Kim, and I were engaged at the time, and the song became almost a theme for our courtship.

Where Are You Going?

A year or so after we were married, Kim and I lived in an apartment on Main Street in Binghamton, a block away from the TV station. One night we were awakened by someone knocking at our third-floor apartment back door. It was a firefighter. The building next door, which was connected to ours, was on fire. We had to get out.

Kim was eight months pregnant at the time. There was a lot of smoke. It didn't seem to me that there was a lot of fire. I said to Kim, "I'll be right back." She said, "Where are you going? You're not leaving me here!" So, I said, "OK, let's go." We walked the block or so to the TV station and got a film camera. We came back, stood on the sidewalk in front of our apartment building, and I took footage of the fire. To this day she loves telling the story of how I was ready to leave her there, pregnant, at 2 a.m. while I went to get a camera to tell a story.

By the way, I left the apartment that night without grabbing my contact lenses or glasses. Most of the footage was unusable. Blurry. The TV station got about twenty usable seconds out of it. Kim has gotten years out of it. When she tells the story, people usually give me a look that says, *Really?*

It is both a blessing and a curse to be bitten by the news bug. It infects you forever!

YOUNGSTOWN

From Binghamton, I moved up to a job as the weekend anchor at WYTV in Youngstown, Ohio. I had sent out dozens of resumes and videotapes of my work. I had received dozens of rejection letters and returned tapes. When WYTV offered me a job, I jumped at it. It was not a great station, but it was a bigger television market. A bonus was that it was close to Cleveland. I was an avid Browns fan. (And despite the pain over all these years, I remain one!)

Youngstown, at the time I arrived there, was mob-infested. For a news guy, that meant it was a great place to learn how to cover a city where you could get some dirt under your fingernails. Problem was, I was the weekend anchor and was only on the streets three days a week. I never got my nails that dirty, but did see a lot from that anchor chair.

There was a huge underworld culture in Youngstown at the time. It was right out in the open. It was almost like the movie *Goodfellas*. People talked with reverence about "Briar Hill Jimmy," the Carabbias, the Strollo Brothers, and Joey Naples. There was a bar and drive-through beverage store close to the TV station, almost out the back door. You could go there to buy beer, pop, and all the usual stuff. You could also go there and play football parlay sheets from your car. In Youngstown, parlays also included high school games. On Tuesday you'd go back and collect if you won.

WYTV aired *Monday Night Football*. If games were in Pittsburgh or Cleveland and didn't sell out, the Youngstown market was blacked out and the TV station couldn't carry the game—which made viewers irate. One Monday night during a blackout, a guy who had been drinking came knocking on the station door, complaining. We didn't want any trouble and he wasn't drunk, just pissed off. We said, OK, come on into the newsroom and watch. We could get the game from ABC; but we couldn't broadcast it. He watched, thanked us, and left. I am sure we had a viewer for life.

That situation gave the photographers an idea. An illegal but ingenious one. On the next blackout night, they cooked up a deal with the bar we backed up to. They ran a cable from the TV station to the bar. The bar then plugged the network football feed into their TVs. They made a fortune because it was the only place in town that had the game. It was on the QT, but all the "goodfellas" in town knew about it. The payoff for the cameraman was a free bar tab for a week or two.

Watch What You Drive to Lordstown

A big employer in the Mahoning Valley at the time was the Lordstown General Motors Plant. Thousands worked there. The UAW was king. It was notorious for a contentious relationship with GM. In the union hall parking lot, there were two parking areas. One was close to the building, with a sign announcing that only American-made cars were welcome there. The other, farther away across a small bridge over a creek, was for anyone driving a foreign car.

Only one of our news vehicles was a foreign make. I don't know how WYTV's station management ever decided to buy it. It was probably a trade-out with one of our advertisers. It wasn't a great move to take that foreign car to a press conference at the union hall. When the crew came out, all four tires were flat. They didn't just leak air. Knife punctures took care of that. Message received. I believe the station bought only American cars after that. They certainly didn't take that foreign car anywhere near Lordstown again.

Donny Osmond

In 1980, just before I moved to Cleveland, I was the co-anchor of the nightly news. One night, the weatherperson was off and we had an opportunity for an unusual replacement. Donny Osmond, "America's Sweetheart" at the time, was in town to promote an upcoming concert given by his family. Arrangements were made to have him come in and do a guest weather segment. I knew a bit about weather and had done the weather in a pinch in the past, so I would lead Donny through it.

The weather segment came, and my co-anchor threw it over to

me. I introduced Donny and announced him as our guest weatherman. In those days, weather graphics were created on a large erasable board showing an outline of the United States. Weather fronts and other information were drawn on the board with a marker by the weather person.

Donny had the marker and started by drawing a big sun over Utah, where his family is from. Good start. He noted that a front had passed us by and that the all-day rain in Youngstown had stopped. I told him he was doing great. Then he moved farther east on the map, and closer to me; then, unexpectedly, he reached over and started drawing the weather on my face!

I was caught flat-footed, dumbfounded. It was unplanned and I was completely unprepared! What was I supposed to do? This was America's Sweetheart; I certainly couldn't punch him. Pushing him away would look awkward; I was at least a foot taller than he was. So I just stood there, going along with it. To this day, I wish I had done something—anything—else.

WELCOME TO CLEVELAND . . . JUST DON'T CROSS "MOTHER"

I APPLIED FOR A JOB in Cleveland multiple times and was always turned down. I even got a lunch interview one time, but was turned down once again. Finally, in 1981, with time running out for me in Youngstown because of bad ratings at the station, I was hired by WEWS, Channel 5 in Cleveland.

Arriving at WEWS was like a dream to me. I was now working in what at the time was a top-ten city in television market size. I was close to my beloved Browns. (And it was a time when press credentials meant simply showing up at the gate with a camera.) And I met some unique TV personalities in Cleveland. Most notable among them was the legendary Dorothy Fuldheim. She was a broadcast veteran who worked into her eighties doing interview shows and nightly commentaries on the 6 p.m. and 11 p.m. newscasts. She was always called Miss Fuldheim to her face. "Mother" was the more familiar term co-workers used when she wasn't around.

In 1981, I was an upstart reporter and 11 p.m. producer at WEWS. Dorothy Fuldheim's commentaries for the late show were supposed to be about a minute and ten seconds. They typically were double that. After a few months of producing the show, I noticed that she usually did two separate topics. Her favorites were President Ronald Reagan, whose name she pronounced *Ree*gan, or the Saudis, which she pronounced Saw-*uu*di's.

One night we had a lot of news to fit in. I needed more time to do it, so I told legendary director Bill "Dad" Wiedenman to dump out of Dorothy's commentary after her first topic. He looked at me in horror and said, "You know you're playing with fire, junior." We clipped her, and nothing was said. It became a regular practice once or twice a week. Then I made a mistake.

Another night, the show was very heavy because of breaking news. "Dad" told me I had to cut two minutes and eleven seconds from the news to fit everything in. This meant cutting ten or fifteen seconds off a bunch of stories. Two other Cleveland legends did the weather and sports, Don Webster and Gib Shanley. There was no cutting them. I noticed that Dorothy was two minutes and eleven seconds long. Bingo! Easy fix, I killed her whole commentary. She didn't find out.

I did this a few more times, depending on news demands. One day, after I had cut Dorothy the evening before, trouble began. I walked into work, and Lou Maglio (later a long-time anchor at WJW), said, "Orlo, you're in some trouble." I asked what he meant. He said "Dorothy." It still wasn't connecting with me. He asked if I had killed her commentary the night before. I had done it so often that I had to think for a moment. I remembered that I had. He had that same look of horror that "Dad" had when I first cut her commentary in half. His eyes widened. "Completely?" he asked. Yes. Apparently, this time she had found out. I knew I was in trouble. Lou told me that she had been looking for me all day and was incredibly angry. I knew she never watched the late news; she was in bed by then. How did she find out? Seems that she had gone out to dinner with friends who were visiting town. They watched the late news and called her in the morning to tell her she had not been on the newscast. I asked Lou to keep his eyes open, and we began writing news copy.

Lou saved me. An hour later I heard him say, "Orlo, she's here." Like a scared child I kicked my chair back and went down on my hands and knees, shielded by my desk. Dorothy was very short, so I knew she couldn't see me. I heard her voice say, "Which one is the producer?" I owe Lou to this day. He stood up and said, "Miss Fuldheim, how are you?" She didn't answer, but sternly asked, "Where is the producer?" Lou didn't say my name or even my nickname, Orlo (which I've always been called in Cleveland). Instead, he said, "Oh, that's the Big O." "Where is the Big O?" Dorothy asked. "He's out on an assignment right now, Miss Fuldheim." I looked up from my hands and knees and gave Lou a thumbs up. She said, "Well you tell the Big O to come and see me when he gets back, or he's fired."

I never went to see her, and eventually she forgot. But not everyone forgot.

Garry Ritchie, the station manager, saw me the next day. "Paul, what is this that I'm hearing—you cut Dorothy?" I told him that I had been doing it when I needed time for breaking news or other stories. His reply was classic; he let out an almost pained, "OOHHH." Next, he asked, "Does Ed know?" Ed Cervenak was the general manager. I said I didn't think so. "Good," Garry said. "Don't ever tell him, and don't ever do it again." He had now covered his tracks in case Cervenak found out. He'd be able to say, "I spoke to him, Ed." That was the way it was back then. No letters of reprimand, no HR department, just people dealing face to face with one another.

This story isn't meant in any way to demean Dorothy's accomplishments. She interviewed all the big ones. Her last interview was President Reagan. One of her first came before television existed, a radio interview with Adolf Hitler. A Jewish woman interviewing Adolf Hitler. Wow!

She interviewed Jerry Rubin, a co-founder with Abbie Hoffman of the Yippie (Youth International Party) movement, a leftist student activism, anti-war group. During the interview, Jerry kept using the term "pigs." At some point Dorothy asked, "Are you referring to animals?" He said, "No, I'm referring to the police." She told him she had many friends who were police officers. He used the term again, and she slammed a book he had brought onto the desk and demanded, "Out!", gesturing toward the door. He looked astonished. She said, "Stop the interview." Out the door he went.

I had a personal view of the power of this woman. The *Cleveland Press* was on its deathbed in 1982. We were trying to confirm that it was about to go out of business, leaving Cleveland as one of the few major American cities with only one daily newspaper. We tried for two days, with no success.

On the second day, a cameraman from the field radioed into the assignment desk that a competing station had a live truck out in front of the *Press* building. We thought we were sunk. In the newsroom, we all watched the 6 p.m. news on all three stations; and no one had the story. Just then, Dorothy entered the newsroom, heading to the studio to do her commentary. "What is going on?" she asked me. I told her that there were rumors about the *Press* folding. "Would you like me to find out?" she asked. I said that would be great. "Get me a telephone," she demanded. Then she dialed a number and said, "Herb Kamm, please." He was the editor of the *Press*. Someone on the other end apparently tried to put her off, but she would have none of it. "It's Dorothy. I must speak to him." She waited about thirty seconds, he answered, and she said, "Herb, is it true?" There was a pause, she slammed her hand down and said, "I must know." After a moment she said politely, "Thank you." She looked at me and said, "It's true." That was power like I had never seen.

She scrapped her scripted commentary and quickly ad-libbed a two-minute commentary that you would have thought took two days to write.

That is the stuff TV news legends are made of!

INVESTIGATING THE POLICE

WHEN I WAS AT WEWS, I began by just looking for feature stories that I could get on the air. Other reporters had established beats. I found I could get my feature stories sandwiched into a newscast that was full of very talented reporters. Over time I got into the mainstream. By the time I had been there for about four years, it was time for a change. Time to reinvent myself. And that meant a move to a different station.

WKYC, which was owned by NBC at the time, had the resources to support longer-term investigative reporting. My time at WKYC began with a fluke tip about cops goofing off. It is one of many stories that didn't make me many friends in the Cleveland Police Department. One stands out above all the rest. It was the story that put me on the map in Cleveland. It also ended up putting me on the NCIC crime computer, a national database of people with outstanding warrants for their arrest.

CAR 224, WHERE ARE YOU?

I received a tip that a lot of Cleveland Police officers and even their supervisors were goofing off at a report room that had been set up for them at Deaconess Hospital on Pearl Road. (Years later, it became a skilled nursing facility.) The report room was intended to be a place where officers could take a break or write reports without having to return to their district headquarters. The Second District is a busy place, and geographically it is the largest district in the city, so the plan made sense. But I was told that it was more of a place to kill a shift or flirt with a nurse.

I carried a note about the tip in my back pocket for a couple of weeks. Then one night we were returning from checking out an accident and drove past the hospital. I had the cameraman pull over. We looked around and saw a couple of police cars at the emergency room, which was not unusual. Then I checked the parking garage. I had been told that many officers parked there to avoid being seen by passing cars. Jackpot. At least a half-dozen police cars were parked there, including supervisors' cars.

We shot a lot of video that night. The next night we returned early and watched as officers spent hours at the hospital. By listened to the police scanner we figured out that once they were on the clock, they would go answer two or three quick calls, and then head to the hospital. When an officer arrived at the hospital, he would radio to dispatch that he and his partner were done with their first call. They really had completed all three. An hour later, they'd radio that they were done with number two. On and on it went. They were time shifting, thereby creating hours of down time.

I knew that this would be a bombshell story, and I didn't want to be unfair to anyone or be criticized for nickel-and-dime stuff. Officers are allowed a thirty-minute break for lunch. We saw lots of cars taking forty-five or fifty minutes. We never mentioned any of them. I thought an hour was fair, but just to be sure, we didn't mention any car or officer that was there for less than an hour and ten minutes—more than double the time allowed. We recorded at the hospital a few more nights.

We had plenty to report on. A couple of cars were there for over five hours at times. Three- and four-hour stops were not uncommon. I reported the story on both a Thursday and a Friday night newscast. The real trouble was about to begin—for me!

THE FAKE TICKETS

Two of the officers involved in (although not actually named in) my stories decided to pay me back. Much later, I figured that they had been angry because I had chosen their car number, 224, for the title of the series of stories. I only chose it because it sounded like the 1960s TV show *Car 54, Where Are You?*

Unbeknownst to me, they wrote three traffic tickets against me—for speeding, running a red light, and almost hitting a pedestrian. One problem: I wasn't anywhere near the intersection where they claimed this happened at the time. The copy of each ticket, which would normally have gone to me, was thrown away because it was a made-up incident. The police copies of the tickets, though, were entered into the system.

I didn't show up for court because I never got the tickets. As a result, an arrest warrant went out for me. I knew nothing of that, either. Sometime later, because of not showing up in court, my name and information were placed on the National Crime Information Center's fugitive list, a nationwide database of fugitives from justice. This meant that if I were in another state and was pulled over, I would be arrested based on this information. I would be in jail for a couple of days until it got sorted out. And I knew nothing of it!

"YOU'RE IN SOME TROUBLE"

Lucky for me, I was never pulled over or got a real ticket. Several months passed. One day, I bumped into a Cleveland city council member as I walked out the front door of the television station. He said, "Hey, you're in some trouble. I just heard there is warrant out for your arrest." *What?* He repeated that there was a warrant out for me, and he told me who told him. He had a good police source. He asked me if I had a lot of tickets. I said no. He suggested that I call the Clerk of Courts.

Still thinking it was a joke, I called the clerk, Benny Bonanno. He laughed, but said he'd check. He came back to the phone and said, "You better get over here." I went to see him, and he said, "Before we get started, sign your name on this piece of paper." It was a blank page, and I obliged. He compared my signature to the signature on the tickets. Not even close. In fact, whoever signed them had misspelled my name. An investigation was immediately launched by the Cleveland Police Department.

Even more frustrating, I could no longer report the story—because I was now the topic of the story. Another reporter at the station picked it up.

THE POLICE INVESTIGATION

To its credit, the Cleveland Police Department launched a major investigation. Within a couple of days, they learned which computer had been used to access my information, who had been in the Second District Headquarters at the time the tickets were written, and who had access to the ticket book that was used. Two officers, partners on Car 224, were identified, suspended, and charged.

The crimes were serious. Forgery for signing my name to the ticket, perjury for swearing that the ticket was true by signing it, falsification of records, tampering with evidence, and uttering. I never knew what uttering was until this happened. (It is entering a document that you know to be false into the legal system.) They entered not guilty pleas and a trial date was set.

THE TRIAL

The first day of the trial was compelling. Handwriting experts testified, along with others. When we showed up for day two, the pair entered guilty pleas to everything. A sentencing was set for a few weeks later.

Then a funny thing happened.

As the day of sentencing approached, I was told that the judge was in a tough spot. If he threw the book at them, he would tick off the Cleveland Police Patrolmen's Association and the Fraternal Order of Police, two powerful police unions. If he went light on them, he might be criticized for showing favoritism to police. Insiders at the court got word to me that he wanted me to speak at the sentencing. It gave me serious pause. The whole situation caused a lot of anxiety. My family was home alone most nights as I worked the evening shift. My wife was understandably worried. What should I do? I gave it a lot of thought.

I showed up for sentencing and saw the two cops in the courtroom. More importantly, I saw their families. Wives and children were crying. In some way, they were victims too. Clearly, the officers would be fired and could never be police officers again, as the crimes were felonies.

The judge did all the formalities, then said, "Is there anyone else that would like to speak?" He was looking directly at me. I raised my hand. "Your Honor, one of these officers has twenty-one years on the job. The other, eleven. I think that if you can find a way to use that experience to help the community that would serve us better than sending them to prison."

They had apologized in court. The newspaper headlines the next day had a box with one of my quotes: "All I ever wanted was an apology, and I got it." That was only half true. I was truly angry at what they had done and how they abused their power. In retrospect, I am glad that I handled it the way I did. They deserved prison. Their families did not. They got probation and were fired. Close to two dozen other officers were disciplined at various levels after the hospital story aired.

A BAD THING TURNED GOOD

Two important things and one funny one came out of the trial. My contract with the station was coming up in a couple of months. The story had been on and off the front page of the Cleveland and Akron newspapers for weeks. When the general manager called me in to negotiate, he said, "How much do you want?" We laughed. I told him. He didn't give it to me, but what I got was still big! Out of some bad things, good things come. And not just the pay raise. I was now "on the map" with the big guys in town, Carl Monday and Tom Meyer of Channel 8's I-Team.

The second important thing is that while the story was a blessing and contributed greatly to my being able to stay on Cleveland television for so long, it also put me into a position I didn't envy. I was now seen as primarily an investigative reporter. I always felt that title was like a lead weight that slowed you down. If a story was an "investigative report," the script would be torn to bits by lawyers and reviewed by so many sets of eyes that in the end sometimes it didn't resemble what you initially set out to report. That also translated to a story taking three days for what you could do in three hours—or three weeks to do what you could do in three days—if it wasn't labeled an "investigative" report.

I tried to avoid the title for years after "Car 224." I did investigations but I tried to keep them quick-hitters. I was always on-air three or more times a week. But that eventually came to an end. I noticed that a new news director liked reporters to have specialties. He had a medical reporter, an education reporter, a City Hall reporter, and more. Reporters without specific areas of expertise were let go. A light went on for me. I went into his office and said, "You know, we should put a name on the investigative work I do." With that, "Target Three" was born. Another reinvention of myself.

The funny thing that came out of "Car 224" is something that anyone who has been married a while can relate to. After the ticket writing was first exposed, my wife said, "We have to get a security system." I said we didn't need a security system. Those were just a couple of rogue cops. She said, "No, we are getting a security system. We are here alone at night while you are at work, and we need a security system." Back and forth we went until we finally reached one of those marital compromises: We got one!

I just thought of another funny element to this story. Several months after the trial, I got a call from one of the two convicted officers. He told me that the city was punishing them by delaying paying what they were owed from monies they had contributed to their pensions. For a moment I thought of hanging up in his ear, but then thought, "Well, that's not fair." It sounded like a good story. I reported the story, and it got them their money. I would have done it for anyone else who was in the same situation as they were, so why not them? Besides, it was December and it probably saved me from going out to stand by the side of the road to tell people it was snowing (my least favorite live shot assignment of all time).

THE ROMPER ROOM

After the "Car 224, Where Are You?" story, tips began to flow about this or that police misdeed. One in particular interested me. It said that a bar owned by a police officer, The Romper Room, was a place where officers not only hung out on the job but also drank on the job. This took the Car 224 story up a notch. Guys with badges and guns don't mix well with booze—not in anybody's book.

Back to the surveillance van we went. We discovered quickly that the tip had been accurate. Police cars were there nightly, even a car driven by a Fifth District supervisor. His district is miles from the bar, located in the Third District. We got good video for a couple of nights. It was time for us to go in and see what was going on. I gave twenty dollars to a couple of the camera guys and they went inside. I stayed in the van with a third camera guy shooting video. Hours went by. Finally, the two camera guys came out. "What took you so long?" I asked. Their weak explanation was that they didn't want to show that they were out of place, so they drank up the entire twenty dollars. A beer those days was about two bucks. They had a load on. Still, they were able to confirm that even with their first beer they saw officers drinking.

I eventually confronted the bar owner and questioned the police chief and a politician or two. Another police department investigation was launched, and another wave of discipline followed. Fourteen officers from the rank of patrolman to captain caught in my investigation were suspended. The bar owner resigned two days after my story (preserving his pension).

The story did not end there.

HIS ATTACKS

I later ran into the officer whom we videotaped, on duty but out of his district at the Romper Room. A couple of guys from the TV station and I went to a sports bar after work. He was not happy to see me, and he bull-rushed me near a side door. I was a lot bigger than he was, so I didn't fall, but I was shocked. He had been drinking, and swore at me as the officers working security led him away.

He wouldn't give it up. One day a few weeks later, I was walking through the Galleria in downtown Cleveland—at the time a vibrant two-story shopping mall. I was on the first floor, going to grab something for lunch. The officer was on the second floor. I didn't see him and only learned he was there after he started shouting, "Look at him down there. Paul Orlousky. He's a piece of s***. Look at him, he's a piece of s***." It was not a comfortable spot for me to be during a crowded lunch hour, but I believe he came off a lot worse than I did to the puzzled shoppers.

HE BLAMED ME, BUT . . .

My story on him, and his treatment of me, weren't totally responsible for his firing. He had a history with the department. I learned after checking his background that years earlier, Cleveland Mayor George Voinovich was taking a group of out-of-town VIPs on a tour of Cleveland aboard the *Good Time II* sightseeing boat. They were heading east along the Lake Erie shorefront, and the mayor was pointing out the sights. Sounds like a nice night, right? Then the normally levelheaded but at times emotional mayor saw something that made him livid.

At the East 55th Street Marina, there was a guy fishing. The problem was that he was a police officer, in uniform, with the trunk of the police cruiser wide open from when he had retrieved his fishing gear. The mayor blew a gasket. Yes, it was the same officer with whom I had had the run-ins after the Romper Room story. It shows my story wasn't all that got him fired.

CREAM PUFF COPS

The most memorable, yet probably the weakest story I ever reported on the Cleveland Police Department (or any police department) is memorable because of the clever title we came up with: "The Cream Puff Cops." Promotion director Dan Klintworth designed an ad campaign that won a national ADDY award.

I had done stories about cops goofing off, even drinking on the job. But a story about cops in a donut shop?

Our general manager regularly parked his car across East 9th Street in a parking garage that had street-level retail. One of the shops was Hough Bakery. Each day the GM would go past and see officers inside the bakery. At times, the officers were carrying trays of baked goods and almost appearing to be hired help. He bugged me for weeks: "You gotta do that Hough Bakery story."

We had done serious stories about goofing off, drinking on the job and even other citizens being falsely ticketed as I had been. This story, though, I avoided like the plague, over and over. I felt that given the prior stories on the fake tickets and the drinking, this would be a step down. The GM insisted, though—eventually telling me he wanted to see it for the upcoming sweeps period. This meant that the story would get a lot of advance promotion before it aired, to drive viewership up during a time when ratings services were measuring viewership.

Sadly, I bowed to the pressure.

Shooting the story was as easy as shooting fish in a barrel. It was all true. We shot it and confronted the officers. The lead officer was Emil Cielek, a man who was a true hero in service to the City of Cleveland. He had been on the force for decades and would have made more money had he retired, rather than continue working. He just loved the job. And he was a great ambassador for the department. He was community policing before it had a title.

Emil and the others were disciplined; nothing serious, a slap on the wrist. I would see him from time to time over the years after the story, and he would always bust my chops, saying, "Oh, this guy busted me." It was usually good-natured and never mean. Over time it got way more friendly. He'd say, "I love this guy. He did a story on me, but I love him." He was a grandfatherly type guy.

At some point, they assigned Emil to the police unit at Cleveland Hopkins Airport. At first, he didn't like it. He had been moved there after refusing to back down from a mayor who didn't like what he found in an accident investigation. This was his punishment. But it was a great job for him because of his ease in talking to people. At the airport, I would see him more often, and we became even more friendly over time.

Emil eventually retired. I learned about it in a phone call from Father John Cregan, the Catholic chaplain of the Cleveland Police Department. "Paul, Emil's retiring, and he'd like to have you come and speak at his retirement party at Brennan's Party Center." I said, "Father, someone is pulling your leg. He and I have a history." He said, "No, he mentioned that. He wants you to come and he wants you to speak." I thought he was crazy or that I was being set up. He assured me it was Emil's desire. I showed up that night and found out I was sitting at a table with Emil and his family. I was uncomfortable at first, but his desire was genuine. He treated me the way he treated everyone else. With kindness.

The first to speak was the leader of the statewide Fraternal Order of Police. He talked about how, wherever he'd go in Ohio, people knew of Emil's legendarily long career. He said it over and over. "Wherever I go, they ask if I know him." He told a couple more stories and it was my turn. What to say?

Emil and I had made peace, but I don't think everyone else in the room was on the same page. Some seemed to wonder, *What the hell is he doing here?* But the FOP guy had given me an opening to break the ice. As I took the microphone I said, "I have a similar story to what you just heard. Wherever I go in the State of Ohio, if his name comes up, I am asked, 'Are you the a**hole who did that bakery story?'" It broke the ice with the crowd. I told a couple of stories about his kind interactions with me after my news story about him. I'll never forget the license plate on his personal car:

STOLAT—a traditional Polish phrase or song that in short expresses good wishes, good health, and a long life to a person.

Emil's retirement came after fifty-plus years on the force. He died a couple of years later.

REGRETS

"Cream Puff Cops" was one story I regretted doing. (And I should have protested more.) But Emil Cielek's kindness in those years after the story was an inspiration on how to approach future stories and people in general.

At some point in every confrontation, when you ask one too many questions or go over the line, you become the jerk, not the person you are confronting. It is a palpable moment. After that moment, it doesn't matter if you are questioning a murderer, a robber, or anyone else. You take their place as the jerk in viewers' minds. People remember your demeanor and forget what the bad guy did. Like anyone, I've failed at times in this, but thanks to this one kindly old guy, I've tried much harder ever since.

SWEEPS

FOR THE BULK OF MY TV career, the most important months of the year were February, May, November, and (to a lesser degree) July. Those were sweeps months—when ratings services closely monitored how many people were watching each station.

When those services published their ratings, the ratings "book," as it was called, showed each station how much they could charge for advertising. Higher ratings translated to higher ad rates.

Sweeps months were so important to television stations that reporters and anchors weren't allowed to take vacation during sweeps months. (They weren't quite so strict in July, which wasn't considered a "major" sweeps month.)

TV stations made a lot of programming decisions based on sweeps. Sweeps drove stations to do stories that were sensational, sometimes way over the top, and sometimes without a lot of news value.

Here are some stories about stories that resulted from competing for ratings during sweeps months.

REST IN PIECES

"Rest in Pieces" was the title for an exposé about a suburban cemetery's questionable cremation practices. It was clever but, I admit, a bit irreverent. It was for a TV ratings period, and I am the one guilty of coming up with the title.

I had a tip that the owner of the cemetery was not completely incinerating human bodies at his crematory. It was 1993, energy costs were high at the time, and it took a lot of extra time and thus energy to burn some of the thicker bones such as hips, leg bones, or clavicles.

The tip came from a worker at the cemetery. He told me that after the remains were reduced to just bones, the incineration process would stop. State law said that "cremains" (as they are known) should be reduced to an unrecognizable form before being returned to a family. If larger pieces of bone remained, they were to be put through a stainless-steel grinder to render them unrecognizable.

That was not being done at this particular cemetery. The tip-sters said that enough of the cremains would be put into an urn to satisfy the family and then the larger bones were simply placed in one of three 55-gallon drums. When all three drums were full, they would be taken to an open grave and dumped into it before the vault for that day's burial was lowered into place. It sounded unbe-lievable to me. Station management almost laughed me out of the room when I told them about it. I reasoned there was nothing to lose except the half-hour to drive there. So when the worker called back, I said, "Show me."

The next day, in the early evening, I went into the crematory along with cameraman Pete Miller. A body was being cremated in a large oven, with intense flames that could only be seen through a small opening as big as a silver dollar. The flames were all you could see. The worker said, "here you go," pointing to a corner. I walked just a few feet, and there were the 55-gallon drums—nearly full of human bones. The bones were clearly recognizable, a hip, clavicle, and what appeared to be a femur. I was shocked. We got a few shots, and I did my stand-up talking about the barrels while holding up and describing three or four of the hundreds of bones we found. It probably wasn't a good idea to handle the bones, but I did it. Great stand-up. When I showed it to our station managers, the story was immediately moved to the lead story for the upcom-ing ratings period. They also practiced "social distancing" with me that day—long before that term became part of the vernacular.

Next came the hard part: proving the rest of the allegation.

It was a ridiculously hot July in Cleveland when our surveillance began. I was with cameraman Greg Lockhart. Our goal was to get video of the drums of bones being dumped. We were in an unmarked van and could open the windows only a crack. It was unbearable. We couldn't have the air conditioning on because the noise would make it obvious we were there. We got soaked with sweat each of the three days we were there. And the weather forecast said it was going to get hotter. I still had to catch the crews dumping the bones on video, but this approach clearly wasn't working.

I called the tipster. "When is the owner going to have you guys dump the bones?" He didn't know. I asked him to call if he got advance notice. Eventually he called, late on a Friday night. There was to be a burial on Saturday morning, and the barrels of bones would be dumped before the vault was put into place. The family of the person being buried would have no idea that dozens of other people's remains were in the same grave. I thought, *What if this were going to be the final resting place for me or a family member?* I bet I know how you would answer that question!

Early that Saturday, cameraman Dan Keefe and I were across the street. Just as predicted, here came a small tractor towing a trailer, and on it were the three drums I had seen a few days before in the crematory. We videotaped as the first drum was dumped. Then, we moved across the street and shot from the sidewalk as the second drum was dumped. As the third drum was being emptied, we walked right up to the grave. Dust from the cremains rose toward the camera lens. Up close, it felt even more disrespectful to the person about to be buried. At the bottom of the grave were old, wilted flowers, grass clippings, and other refuse. Disgusting.

Next, we headed to the office to find the owner.

We found him and confronted him. He was a crusty old guy who denied everything in no uncertain terms. I told him we had taped it, and he denied it again. I said, "Come on, I'll show you." I met him at the grave and pointed out the mess at the bottom. He tried to blame the workers, saying he didn't know anything about it. It was an unconvincing claim, given that he was the person who operated the crematory's incinerator and was responsible for the barrels of bones.

In the days after the story, I questioned legislators and regulatory agencies about the practice we had documented. There was a short discussion in the state legislature, but nothing happened.

This is the kind of story that frustrates you as a reporter. I felt it was a great service to inform people of this outrageous practice, and it seemed that some regulation or law should be changed. Possibly a sanction against the owner was in order. Yet nothing happened. Maybe I should have pushed harder in the days after the story. I've always felt bad that I didn't.

WEST VIRGINIA BLUES

In 1986, the Associated Press released a government report saying that the state of West Virginia had, essentially, no future because its coal mines were depleted, its terrain was difficult for commerce, education was lagging, and people were leaving in droves. The premise of the AP story was that it was doomsday there.

The story didn't have much to do with Cleveland, but news director Ron Bielek thought it would work for sweeps. Not one to just have you simply recite quotes from a report like this on the air, Bielek called me into his office and said, "I want you to go to West Virginia and see how these people are living."

Cameraman Ron Strah and I traveled to a town in one of the counties mentioned in the AP report, near the Ohio border. After checking into a hotel, we drove out through some backwoods areas. There, we found exactly what the AP report said. At one point, we stopped at a home that looked like the one the Beverly Hillbillies had lived in before moving to Beverly Hills—the home in the opening scene from the TV series. Wood-heated, smoke coming out of the chimney, a woman cooking over a wood fire . . . The owner asked us if we wanted to try some squirrel gravy because he had just been out hunting and got a few. "It's real good on your 'taters," he told us. We declined.

I'm not here to knock West Virginia. We stayed in a very nice hotel in a pleasant town. All was not gloom and doom. But there was plenty of doom. In one town we visited, the only remaining job was the postmistress. One job in the entire town!

On our second night in West Virginia, we went to a rural bar. The premium beer on tap was Old Milwaukee. We asked people about living there, and they shared tragic stories. One man could tell us exactly the time and date that he had "swung my last hammer for the railroad." It was more than ten years earlier, and he hadn't had a job since. Behind him and a brightly lit pool table, a large hound dog jumped to grab a piece of meat dangled in front of him.

Feeling that we had a bond with a few of the patrons, I began to ask more probing questions about the AP report, which had mentioned incest and other kinds of abuse. This didn't go over well—it was sort of a biker bar—and pretty soon Ron and I figured that we had about ninety seconds to leave. We left!

Ron had the idea to shoot the entire story as postcards, and that is what he did. Ron, editor Ann Ruhlin, and I all won Emmy awards for the stories. It was a clever way to cover the story. And the story was a ratings hit. But I was left with the feeling that we had used those people's plight for our own purposes. However, in TV news, when the boss says "go and do it," you go and do it.

LOCKSMITHS

A caller said that we should check out locksmiths. He claimed that many of them didn't ask for much identification before busting a lock and giving someone access to a house, a car, or other facility. It was May 1992. Sweeps were approaching, and I needed a promotable story. I came up with a plan. Our story would be split into three parts: first, a woman supposedly locked out of her home; then, a woman locked out of her car; finally, a veterinary tech who said she was locked out of an animal clinic. Each story escalated the possible danger. The house would be a simple burglary, if the person asking to get in had criminal intent (we did not). The locked car would have been a grand theft auto. The veterinary clinic stored narcotic drugs.

I had a woman from our assignment desk sit on the front porch of photographer Ron Strah's home. She was looking forlorn when the locksmith showed up, and complained that her husband was out of town and she hadn't been able to get in touch with anyone who could help her. She told him she knew exactly where the keys to her (actually, Ron's) car and home were located inside. The locksmith was suspicious at first, but she told him that she had just locked herself out on the way to work. She said the keys were on the arm of a chair that couldn't be seen from the porch. He jimmied the lock, let her in and she led him to the chair saying, "See—here they are." He was satisfied, and she paid him.

And it was on to our next scenario.

We parked a car in the lot of Westgate Mall and purposely locked a set of keys inside. (We had a second set in case things didn't work out.) We called a nearby locksmith that we found in the phone book. (Remember those?) He came out and checked out the situation. Without asking for any identification, he tried to jimmy the lock but had no luck. "Well, I'm gonna have to drill it out," he told our decoy. This was a problem because the car belonged to Bob Tayek, one of the news managers at the station, and he wouldn't appreciate his car being ruined. Our decoy made a bunch of excuses not to drill the lock. Eventually, the locksmith tried another tool, fished and fiddled with it, and managed to open the car door. Disaster averted.

The final test was at a veterinarian's office. It was a vet my wife and I used for our pets—a good guy who in advance gave me great background on the kinds of drugs stored inside that could easily be abused by a human. The decoy stood out front and gave the locksmith a reasonable sounding excuse as to why she was locked out. The locksmith said there wasn't much he could do. She told him how the place would be closed for the weekend and the animals would have no care. She might get fired. He made a new key and let her in.

Every company we called came and did what we asked. No one said no. It was that easy. We never did a confrontation with any of the three locksmith companies. Our intention wasn't to jam any one of them or all of them. Our aim was to change protocols in these situations by locksmiths—or at least make people aware of what could happen. I don't see stories like this on the news much anymore.

ASLEEP AT THE SWITCH

Workers sleeping on the job is ratings magic. So when I got a call that one of the operators of the West Third Street lift bridge on the Cuyahoga River came to work every night and went to sleep after about an hour on duty, there was no question I was going to do the story. Besides, the bridges on the river are more than a hundred years old and need to be manned twenty-four hours a day to maintain traffic on the river for the large ore boats that supply the steel mills upriver. There was less traffic on the overnight shift, but still, the bridges had to be ready.

Sleeping-on-the-job stories were hard to capture on video. Cameraman Ed Verba and I got to the bridge at about 11 p.m. Just before midnight, a car pulled up and parked near the bridge. A man got out carrying a boom box, a blanket, a large bag of chips, and a pillow. He climbed up into the control room of the bridge, and the previous operator left. Just as we were told, about an hour later out went the lights. They never came back on.

Ed and I waited there until dawn and then quietly climbed up on the bridge. Inside the control room, the operator was lying on a cot. He was out like a light. We shot video of him for a minute or so, and then I knocked on the door frame. He jumped up quickly while the cot squeaked loudly (which made the visual better). "Hi, Channel 3," I said. "Sure looked like you were sleeping." He said that he hadn't been. I said, "We've been here a while, and you were definitely sleeping." He explained that he closed his eyes for a few minutes.

The next part, I'll never understand. I asked if anything like this had ever happened before. He said, "Yeah, I was disciplined last year for it." I was dumbfounded. I never expected an answer, let alone that one. I almost wanted to say, *Dude, you don't* have *to answer my questions.*

The operator was disciplined with just a suspension. The person who tipped me off was also a bridge operator. After the story—"Asleep at the Switch"—aired, the City of Cleveland ordered all cots, couches, stuffed chairs, and television sets removed from the control rooms. The tipster, too, had to suffer the correction of the problem. He didn't talk to me for two or three years after that.

YOU NEVER KNOW WHAT
THE DAY WILL BRING

A CHRISTMAS STORY

It was just a routine story to cover at WEWS. Not a lot of fanfare had been made about it. A movie was being made on downtown's Public Square. It was a bit unusual at the time, as not many movies were shot in Cleveland in the early 1980s.

The last big one had been *The Deer Hunter*, in the mid-1970s, which used exteriors of St. Theodosius Cathedral in the Tremont neighborhood. (Much of that movie was shot in Pittsburgh, with a shot or two filmed in Youngstown.) In 1977, interiors of the penthouse at a building then known as the Chesterfield, on East 12th Street near Chester Avenue, were used for a scene in *The Gathering* featuring actor Ed Asner. The movie-making scene in Cleveland had been dry since then.

The new movie being filmed in Cleveland was *A Christmas Story*, adapted from a book by Jean Shepherd. Yes, the same movie that is now a classic holiday ritual for so many.

The movie company made a deal with the City of Cleveland to purchase late 1930s- era Christmas decorations for Public Square if the city would agree to keep the decorations displayed until movie filming was done in February. The city quickly said yes, as the decorations from past years had outlived their usefulness.

Christmas came and went, and the movie crew moved in that January. My assignment was to cover a big parade scene that was to be shot at night. It is the scene where Ralphie looks into a store window display and falls in love with the idea of getting an "Official Red Ryder Carbine Action Two Hundred Shot Range Model Air Rifle" for Christmas.

It hadn't been a particularly cold winter in Cleveland, so the snow you see in the movie was heavily augmented with soap bubbles as a kind of filler. Many locals who owned vintage cars from that era were involved. Modern phone booths were covered by postwar-looking bus stops. A gospel choir from a historic Black Cleveland church is the one singing in the parade. All went well. (I have seen old tapes of my coverage from that night; I was about thirty and looked like a child myself with my excitement.)

A day or two later, I went inside the Higbee department store to interview Peter Billingsley, the actor in the role of Ralphie. It was Higbee's store window that Ralphie was looking into on the corner of Euclid and Ontario when he obsessed on the Red Ryder BB gun. Between two escalators was the Santa Mountain made famous in the movie. The place where Ralphie at first couldn't spit it out, then while being tossed down the slide on the mountain by an elf, stops and asks Santa for the Red Ryder. The spot where Santa listens and says, "You'll shoot your eye out, kid." (By the way, that Santa Mountain elf who sits the kids on Santa's lap is from Cleveland. And yes, I have a leg lamp!)

At the top of Santa Mountain, I interviewed Peter Billingsley, who played Ralphie. I always kind of dreaded doing kid interviews; but he was particularly good. Over the years, I have met many of, and even worked with one of, the children waiting in line to see Santa in the movie. They were local extras. Most were young and don't have a lot of memories of the filming. Elisa Olgin, whom I worked with at WOIO, remembers that Billingsley was "very nice" and that they had a great place to hang out between scenes. She said, "Even had pinball machines and stuff like that, that Peter liked."

The movie didn't do much at the box office. Years later, though, the TBS television network picked it up for its now-annual Christmas Eve and Day marathon, which made it into a classic.

Some of the actors from the movie returned to Cleveland over the years to sign autographs and make appearances. My favorite was Zack Ward, who played bully Scut Farkus. In the first return appearance by the cast, I did a story about it. I had to think of a creative way to "tease" ahead to the story, which would air later in the news broadcast after the first commercial break or two. I had Zack put his arm around my neck from behind, kind of a choke hold. He did that Scut Farkus growl, and I said, "All these years later, and he's still a bully. I'll explain." He was a good sport to play along with us.

ETHNIC GUY

I had been in Cleveland for only a year when I was walking on Public Square one day. From some distance away, I heard an older man with a thick accent yell, "Orlousky." I waved and said hello. TV viewership was very strong in those days. Even after a short time in a new city, people recognized you. The man answered by saying, "I'm Orlousky too." I moved closer and said, "I bet you don't spell it the same way." He said, "You're damn right. Nobody ever misspelled it until you got to town. Now they see that Y at the end of your name on the TV and everybody gets mine wrong." His was spelled *-ski*. You gotta love those old ethnic folks. You never had to wonder what they were thinking. They told you.

BP IMPLOSION

Sometimes you just can't think of all the aftereffects while covering a story. When BP decided to build its US headquarters in Cleveland on Public Square, it required the demolition of two buildings: the Cuyahoga Building and the Williamson Building. Those buildings would be imploded. When the day came, all the news cameras gathered across the square on the roof of a hotel. The countdown came. The explosives began to pop, and down the buildings came. Then, a huge cloud of dust began billowing—directly toward the cameras. It became dark as night for a few moments. That temporary darkness wasn't the real problem. The issue was that the dust got into the camera's zoom lenses. Now, when the photographer tried to zoom or focus, we'd hear a grinding noise. I think just about every camera there had to be sent back to the factory for a good cleaning. If anyone had thought it through, a simple garbage bag would have saved the day. Live and learn!

DETROIT PLANE CRASH

Another time I didn't plan ahead appropriately was when news broke that a plane had just crashed in Detroit. The local Detroit stations were too busy covering the story for their own stations to cover it for NBC, so the network called my station. Cameraman Ron Strah and I were on the west side of Cleveland, so we were the closest to Detroit. Off we went. We weren't prepared for the weather and hadn't planned to be out for hours in the cold. My job was to do live hits for the NBC stations in New York, Washington, Chicago, and Los Angeles. It involved standing on top of a live truck for hours. The temperature was dropping, and on an airfield with nothing to block the wind, it was almost painful. My reward was frostbite on the tip of one of my fingers from holding the metal microphone. Probably should have stopped on the way there and bought some gloves.

DICK FEAGLER AND THE PAGEANT MOMS

I was assigned a lightweight news story about mothers preparing their daughters for beauty contests and talent pageants. No problem. It was part of my "Page Two" segment at WKYC, Channel 3. The second part of the segment was going to be filled by legendary Cleveland journalist and commentator Dick Feagler. I did my segment about the costumes, the makeup, the lessons, and other stuff the girls did to prepare. Next, I threw to Dick, back in the studio, for commentary. He proceeded to deliver a two-minute attack on the whole topic: "When these girls get their fangs sharpened enough to tear each other apart, then they'll be ready for the national pageants. Their moms seem to be giving them a real heads-up in that regard." That was just a bit of what he said. Problem was, I had to stand there waiting for Dick to finish so I could end the segment and say thank you—and I was in the same room with all the girls' mothers, who had been watching Dick's commentary with great intensity. Now they were watching me with something far different than intensity. If looks could kill! I made another quick exit.

A PEPPER GRENADE REALLY STINGS

A man barricaded himself inside an upstairs apartment on East 152nd Street. The standoff went on for hours, and negotiations were unsuccessful. Finally, police decided it was time to get him out. After dark, they launched small grenades with pepper gas into the building, then, wearing masks, rushed in quickly and made the arrest. I did not cover the story but did follow-ups.

The next day the landlord who had rented the apartment to the man called us to complain that the police had torn his place apart. I went there to see. He was right. Beds were turned over, drawers pulled out of dressers and tossed on the floor, and a lot more. I talked to the landlord, and we shot the mess. I still had to do an on-scene "stand-up." I spotted one of the plastic grenades on the floor, and thought that would make a good prop. (Never forget: television is all about pictures, and props help tell a story.)

Cameraman Marty DeChant started rolling, and I held the spent grenade up to the camera explaining what it was. No problem. We left and went to the car. Then I made a big mistake. I rubbed my eyes. The chemical from the grenade was on my hand. Now it was in my eyes. It burned. Better said, it hurt!

I ran back inside the downstairs apartment where the owner lived and asked where the sink was. He pointed and I ran to it. I washed my eyes out over and over. It took several hours before everything was back to normal. Another bad. On me.

ANOTHER BARRICADED GUY

We were on the West Side of Cleveland one night in a nice middle-class neighborhood of bungalows. A man had barricaded himself in his home, along with his disabled brother. Police had gone to his home for some reason, and he wouldn't let them in. At some point he fired a shot and the police retreated. SWAT was called in. Now, the man was threatening to burn the place down, so the Cleveland Fire Department was called in.

The hostage negotiator was there, trying to make a connection with the guy. Using a bullhorn, he'd say, "John, come out. We want to talk to you." The answer was always the same from the home: "F*** you." The negotiator tried many approaches like, "John, I want to be your friend, let's talk." Same answer: "F*** you." This went on for hours. It was almost comical. Especially when the negotiator, who finally thought he had an opening to connect with the man, said, "John, my name is Roger. Come out and talk to me." The reply from inside changed: "F*** you, Roger."

CONFRONTATIONS

Confrontations are a part of the job, at times necessary because there is just no other way to get both sides of a story. I went to a house once to try to find a guy accused of a crime. The main wooden door to the house was open behind the screen door, which was closed. I knocked on the screen door, and someone from another room in the distance said, "Who is it?" I said, "19 Action News." In a terribly angry voice, I heard, "Get the f*** off my porch." As usual, a pit bull had come to the door first and was growling at me. My foot was firmly planted on the screen door to prevent it from opening. I continued, "It's Paul Orlousky." From inside I heard, "Hey, Paul Orlousky is on the porch." A guy came to the door and said, "You *are* Paul Orlousky." He quieted the dog down and talked to me.

Another story was similar, but with a different ending. Marty and I were on the porch of a home. I had just knocked on the door when a guy passing by in a car rolled down the window and said, in a Scooby-Doo imitation, "Ruh-roh." Marty and I were caught off guard and laughed hard. Just then, the guy we were looking for answered the door. I had to get serious fast and didn't pull it off very well. The guy slammed the door in my face.

A QUICK RECOVERY

At a Cleveland School Board meeting, we were there to cover an issue being discussed. My cameraman, Steve Pullen, noticed that one board member, Stanley Tolliver, who was rather elderly, appeared to be asleep. Sooner or later the board would have to vote on the issue, and we wondered if Mr. Tolliver would respond. Finally, the time came for a vote. Each member answered yes or no to the question. When it got to Tolliver, the clerk said, "Mr. Tolliver. Mr. Tolliver." No answer. Then his name was called a third time. His head popped up from resting on his chest and Tolliver said, "Madam Clerk, I was just cogitating on the matter." It was classic Stanley Tolliver. He was a real gentleman who always treated me kindly.

HOW IS A FIRE HYDRANT FUNNY?

I got a tip that the Cleveland Water Department had installed a fire hydrant right in the middle of a sidewalk. Hard to believe anyone would do that. Marty and I took a ride out to the spot and, sure enough, it was true. Turns out, the crew had been told to move the hydrant a certain distance from the street. As they had been ordered to do, they ripped the old sidewalk out, moved the hydrant, and then poured new concrete around it. No room for a baby carriage to pass by, not even a tricycle. I never could get a straight answer on who gave the instructions to do it that way. We aired a story, and the problem was fixed. I don't know the cost, but I do know who paid for this blunder: taxpayers, as usual. (For those in Elmira, yes, it was a Kennedy Valve.)

OHIO LOTTERY TAMPERING

While covering crime stories, I often marvel at the way the criminal mind works. Once, I got a tip from a woman in Canton. She believed that the Ohio Lottery's "Sweet 16" game was fixed. It was a second-chance game in which you had to mail in sixteen losing tickets. Your envelope would then be entered for a drawing to win one of sixteen $1,000 cash prizes. She had kept detailed records showing that one man had won seven times—an unbelievable three times in one week, and twice in another. More than a million entries came in every week. How was that possible?

I went to a Case Western Reserve University professor who had written a book on probability. He said the odds were the same as picking your name at random out of a phone book that was twelve feet thick or flipping heads on a coin twenty-five times in a row. He said it suggested a two-headed coin.

We aired the story, and the next day my phone rang. It was a worker who had the inside scoop. The man who had won all the cash was a postal worker. The caller had watched lottery workers come to the post office and draw winning envelopes out of the bags of entries that had been sent in. He noticed something interesting: They weren't mixing up the entries. Classic laziness. They'd just go to a bag and draw one or two envelopes off the top. He told me that his coworker had seen it, too. It was the guy who won the Sweet 16 all those times. He'd sneak into the room where the bags were kept and just put his entries on top. Clearly it worked.

We went to the Ohio Lottery to get an answer. I was told that the drawings were taped, so I asked to see them. Turns out the tapes were either blank, partial, or too fuzzy to see. The Ohio Highway Patrol launched an investigation, and new safeguards were put into place.

By the way, the same postal worker also had appeared on the Ohio Lottery's *Cash Explosion* TV show and won a new car. After our news story, though, his luck ran out.

BAD WEATHER

TV news loves bad weather. I laughed one time when I was the lead story on a bad snowstorm. The message to viewers from our weather people was, "Don't even think about going out. Stay in your home." That was followed by the anchor saying, "We sent Paul Orlousky on a three-state tour to survey what is going on . . ." Wait, what?

On the way to Cleveland Hopkins airport, cameraman Tom Livingston and I shot some video of local bad weather. We landed in Cincinnati, where the airport is located across the Ohio River in Kentucky, and shot some video of bad weather there. Two states down! Next it was on to Huntington, West Virginia, which was hardest hit. As the plane was approaching the airport and we were just about to land, the engines suddenly revved and we climbed back into the sky. The pilot came on the intercom. "We're going to come around again. There was a snowplow on the runway." I looked at Tom and asked, "Don't they have radios at this place?" We landed and got our story. But the assignment desk hadn't checked the flight schedule. There was no return flight. They had to send a charter plane to get us. It arrived and we made it back to Cleveland just in time for the 11 p.m. news.

DEVIL'S NIGHT IN DETROIT

Cameraman Tom Livingston and I were sent to Detroit the night before Halloween for what was known locally as "Devil's Night." It had become a problem, with arson fires set in abandoned homes, garages, or other structures. Problem was, the flames often jumped from the abandoned structures to homes where people still lived. The fire department couldn't keep up with it.

We went to shoot video at a central dispatch area of about fifty or more fire trucks lined up on the street. They were from all over the city. One by one as the fire calls came in, they were handed their assignments and off they went. When they were done, they'd come back and park at the end of the line, ready to go again. We followed a couple of them, saw the devastation, and talked to people affected. Then, we had to quickly get on a plane to return to Cleveland before the 11 p.m. news. A live truck was waiting for us at the airport. We fed a story back to the station, and I did a live shot. During the live shot, I held up the jacket I had been wearing and said, "This jacket holds the stench of an inner city burning." Good line, right? Until the next year.

The next year we went back to Detroit to cover Devil's Night again. At a press conference held to urge local media not to over-state the problem, Detroit Mayor Coleman Young showed my story and pointed at the screen. "This is not the image we want the rest of the nation to see." I was *persona non grata* even though the story showed exactly what had happened.

We went to WDIV, Channel 4, where Mort Crim was the anchor-man, to feed our early story back to Cleveland. They acted like we carried a disease. But while we were editing our piece, one of their cameramen ran into the newsroom holding a tape over his head saying excitedly, "I got the first fire!" WDIV led with it on their broadcast. They treated me like crap and now that? I just shrugged it off.

I do have to say that Mayor Coleman Young may have been on the right track pointing out the bad publicity Detroit was getting in other cities. It turned out that the number of fires had peaked the previous year, and they diminished every year after that.

REPORTERS BEHAVING BADLY

"WE CAN NEVER TELL ANYONE"

I had a tip from an employee of a local business who claimed that management had hidden a camera in a ceiling fan in the bathroom. I decided to go and check it out. It looked to me like there was something there, but I couldn't tell what it was. The sink wasn't supported well enough for me to climb up on it to get a closer look. We left.

I waited for the guy to call back. He did, and I asked him if he could put a ladder or something else in the bathroom that I could get on top of to get a better look. A day or two later, he called back and said he had put a large container in the bathroom for me. I headed back to the establishment, along with cameraman Pete Miller, who had a camera stuffed in his jacket. Upon entering the bathroom I discovered that the "large container" the guy promised was a five-gallon plastic bucket. Not what I expected. It was only about eighteen inches high and very narrow. No matter; we continued.

Pete pulled the camera out and began rolling. I stood on the bucket and reached up to move a panel of the drop ceiling to try to look above it. I must have leaned too far. The can went out from under me. My reflexes were to grab something. I did: the drop ceiling. The entire ceiling came down on me. Somehow, I landed on my feet. Pete caught it all on tape. The noise was very, very loud. The tape showed a look of horror on my face. "Pete, let's get out of here; act like nothing happened," I said.

We left without running, calmly got in the car, and drove off and parked a few blocks away. I was bleeding from a cut caused by a sharp metal strip of the drop-ceiling frame. And I had a bump growing on my forehead. Apparently, over the years employees had stashed whiskey bottles up above that drop ceiling. One of them had whacked me in the head when the ceiling came down. Neither of us said a word to the other. Finally, I said, "Pete, we can never tell anyone about this." Pete was a pro. "Tell anyone about what, Orlo?" I never mentioned it to anyone until the establishment went out of business and after Pete died.

TOO LOUD

Times have changed the TV business. In the 1970s and '80s, TV station general managers kept fully stocked bars in their offices and there was a refrigerator in either the newsroom or the studio stocked with beer. No one abused it. When your story was done, or after the show, we'd crack open a beer and share stories. It was camaraderie. It wasn't a bad thing, but it is unthinkable today.

In 1982, the United Auto Workers union Local 122 went on strike at the Chrysler stamping plant in Twinsburg. The strike went on for a long time. Eventually, Chrysler ran out of parts, and the entire company was shut down.

Labor and management were negotiating, and on one Friday night there was a marathon negotiating session scheduled for a Holiday Inn in Boston Heights, south of Cleveland. As reporters, we told our audience what we knew about the negotiations—which wasn't very much—on the early news. The two sides broke for dinner, and so did the reporters. We reporters all knew one another and went down to the bar together for a burger and a beer (or two). By 7 p.m., we were back in the hallway outside the room where the negotiations were taking place. While we waited, we entertained ourselves by swapping inflated stories about our exploits and had a great time.

Nothing was happening with the negotiations, so from time to time, two or three of us would head back down to the bar, making sure to never leave the story uncovered. We had each other's backs, and did a rotation among ourselves. It was getting late. We reported the lack of progress on our 11 p.m. stories and were told to stay all night by our news managers. The story was getting national attention, too, so each of us also did phone reports for the overnight network radio news.

At about midnight, the bar closed. We figured we'd be there all night, and we needed another source of beer. We all pitched in money, and I was chosen to go to the nearest corner gas station to buy it. I was picked because the UAW's president, Bob Weissman, knew that reporters at my station at the time were non-union. He wouldn't talk to me, so even if something happened while I was gone on the beer run, I wouldn't miss out on an interview. My cameraman could catch what he said to the others.

As we continued to wait, and drink beer, we started getting loud. At about 3 a.m., a Boston Heights police officer arrived. "They can't get any negotiating done," he said. "You guys are making too much noise. You gotta go downstairs."

We complied. A huge national strike possibly lengthened because we reporters were having a good time!

EAST CLEVELAND PIT BULLS

Marty and I had been covering a situation on a nearly abandoned street in East Cleveland. Refuse haulers and others were using the street as their personal junkyard to avoid paying to have the stuff disposed of at a legal recycler or dump. The few residents who still lived on the street woke up most mornings to large piles of garbage, old tires, and construction debris dumped in their front yards.

We had aired a couple of stories on the garbage and as a result the residents had gotten some relief from the problem. But then the dumping started again.

An energetic but naïve young man at our station who was managing our new live web and Facebook feeds was champing at the bit to come with us. We agreed.

We got to the street in East Cleveland and shot video, starting at the news car and venturing out onto the various properties. At one point, I said to Marty, "Couple of pit bulls over there, Marty," just calling it to his attention. We always had one another's back. The young guy laughed. "You're just trying to get me," he said. "No," I answered, "those are pit bulls running loose. But they won't bother us; they're all over the place in East Cleveland." The young guy looked at me and his smile faded fast and color drained from his face. He slowly backed up toward the van and then got in. Marty and I continued to shoot. Despite the fresh dumping, we found that our stories had caused the City of East Cleveland to clean up much of the mess. It wasn't great, but it was better.

Regarding those pit bulls: When you've spent a lot of time on city streets, you start to get an instinct for when you are safe and when you are not. I hope we taught the young guy a lesson by understanding that and continuing to shoot. Had we sensed danger, we would have been in the car with him. Still, if you watch seasoned investigative reporters when they approach homes in certain neighborhoods, you'll notice they always have one foot blocking the screen door. I know I always did. A big dog can crash right through it if it isn't blocked.

ONE QUESTION TOO MANY

This time I didn't mean to act badly. But Cleveland Police spokesman Bob Bolton sure thought I did. We went to a home where a body had been found hanging in a closet. A couple of things are important in this. If it was a suicide, we leave. We don't cover them unless the person has hurt someone else or disrupted public activity—such as a person jumping off a building downtown.

At this scene, police weren't saying much. So of course all the gathered reporters were curious, asking a lot of questions. Spokesman Bolton didn't give us a reason to leave or a reason to stay. His explanation of the circumstances was vague. I continued to ask questions because I didn't understand what was going on. Should I stay, in case it was a crime, or should I leave because it was a suicide?

The other stations were still rolling, but by now I was the only one still asking questions. I just wasn't getting it. Bolton finally blurted out, "Jesus Christ, Orlousky, he was jerking off while hanging himself." I had never heard of autoerotic asphyxiation before. I now learned—to the chuckles of the other reporters and to Bolton's frustration. I left.

THE KIDDIE PORN KING

A man had been arrested at his apartment complex by Ohio's Internet Crimes Against Children task force (ICAC) for having child pornography on his computer. The online porn led ICAC to discover other crimes. Horrible ones, sex crimes against children, at his apartment complex.

He had been locked up for a week or so when I learned he was being moved from one jail to another. A police source told me the transfer would happen in the afternoon. I got to the police station and waited, and after an hour or so, out came a cruiser. It parked for a moment, and as I approached, the officer lowered his window. I asked him, "Is that so-and-so?" He smiled and said nothing, but pushed the button to lower the back-seat window, giving Marty a full view of the guy, who now was lying down, hiding his face on the seat. I asked him a couple of questions. He didn't answer. I said, "If I give you a piece of candy and a cookie, will you talk to me?" His hands were cuffed behind his back, which was about all we could see; he raised his middle finger in a one-finger salute. The cop laughed and drove off.

I make light of it, but only in that one portion of the story. It was a horrific case. I talked to the detective who led the investigation afterward, and he told me he had nightmares about it. Looking at all the evidence that he had to review for trial made him start smoking again. He was angry and irritable and couldn't sleep some nights. The people who do that job as well as the ICAC members give up a lot of their personal space to do a professional job.

Another aside: In court at kiddie porn trials that I have covered (thankfully there have only been a few where video was played), I am very good at knowing when the perverted images are going to come up. I turn my head, and only when it seems that it is over do I look up. It always worked, except once: I looked up a split-second too soon and caught a brief image of what the poor jurors were forced to watch. It is burned into my mind forever. I cannot get it out of there. It is clear to me that this stuff can rot a weak person's mind. I wish I had waited a split-second more before looking up!

SPREADING GERMS

A new company had purchased WKYC from NBC, and their approach to news was much softer than what I had been doing with my "Target Three" unit. The unit was me and an answering machine, and a cameraman when needed.

I had been doing hard news—the police goofing off, illegal dog fighting, and similar topics. Their big idea for the ratings period was "Is there Unsafe Bacteria on Your Kitchen Dish Rag?" (A similar story had done well during the ratings at another station owned by the company, so they slated it for our ratings sweeps.)

Not what I was used to, but I thought, *OK, I'll play ball.*

My version of the story was intended to show how germs can spread in the work environment. I located a testing kit designed specifically for what we were going to do. It had a powder that could only be seen under a black light. Then, I talked a boss of a small company into letting us into his office before work hours. I put some of the dust on a phone, a desk, a keyboard, and a couple of door handles. We left, and came back a couple of hours after the business opened for the day.

I wasn't prepared for what happened next. I told everyone

involved what we had done. No one had a problem with it. We turned off the lights and I made my way around the room with a little portable black light that came with the kit. It made the powder glow. The powder had been spread everywhere. Then I got the bright idea to scan the workers. It was a bad idea.

The first guy I scanned had it on his hands—but not just his hands. He clearly had been picking his nose. The powder glowed bright blue around his nostrils. He couldn't see it, but all the other workers could, and laughed. He didn't know why. The next guy was one of those who had been laughing very loudly. His turn to be scanned. Nose was clear, and I continued down his body. I got to his waist and headed lower. His crotch glowed bright blue; he had clearly been itching or scratching himself. My reaction was a loud, "Oh," as I pulled the black light away quickly. Everyone saw it. Now, the guy with the blue nose was laughing the hardest. I had a reaction on my face too—it was beet red.

Not my kind of investigative reporting. It was time for yet another reinvention of myself. I decided it was time for a change and had my attorney call the other stations to inquire about their interest. WOIO was very interested, and we hammered out a deal. When WKYC wanted to renew my contract, we declined. It was a bit sticky. The new owners of WKYC weren't aware that my contract was the old NBC boilerplate, which did not contain a non-compete clause that later became commonplace. They weren't happy, but I was thankful for thirteen years there.

THE DUI RECORD HOLDER

This is another serious story where I got the finger. I don't mean to make light of it. A guy who had multiple DUIs and a lifetime license suspension just kept driving. He was near the top of Ohio's list with well over a dozen DUIs. He got another one and hurt someone. We were the in-your-face 19 Action News brand at the time, so as he was led out of court into a sheriff's car, I asked a couple of questions, which he didn't answer. I noted that deputies put him into the back seat of a cruiser, where a third deputy was behind the wheel waiting to take him away. An idea came to me. I thought of a question. "Is this the first time you've ever used a designated driver?" I asked. No answer again. He hunkered down in the back seat, face down, and gave me the finger. Again, even though cuffed with his hands behind his back.

THE HEADLINER

The Headliner, a family owned bar, was located a block or so away from the Cleveland *Plain Dealer* for six decades. It was a hangout for PD reporters, mailers, drivers, and in some cases, bosses. Back in the 1980s, every night at 10 p.m., one side of the bar had to be cleared so the bartender could set up drinks for the union workers involved in the printing of the paper. They only got a ten-minute break, so the bar's owner, Bill "Red" Pigg, had to be ready for them. They were regulars. Joe always sat at the first stool; he got a beer and two shots. Bill sat at the next; he got two beers and a shot. On it went down the line. They would come in, drink quickly, and go back to the paper to use heavy printing machines and even drive trucks. (Clearly this would not be tolerated today.)

Later in the evening, the place became the domain of print reporters. When TV folks started going there, some of the older veteran newspaper reporters didn't like it. They saw us as journalistic lightweights. They claimed the bar as their turf, so we took a pitcher of beer (three bucks!) into a second room.

Over the years our relations became more cordial, and we mingled. As a result, I got some good tips from newspaper reporters who said too much about a story after drinking one too many. Nev Chandler helped break the ice. A legend in Cleveland, a sports anchor at WEWS, and the voice of the Cleveland Browns, Nev could tell a story like no one else, and the newspaper guys loved it. He would come in the back door on Monday nights after a Sunday Browns loss and predictably throw his hands up into the air saying, "Unbelievable." Then he'd dissect the game for everyone.

Over time, the production of the paper became more auto-mated, and in 1994 production operations were moved from downtown to a new, mostly automated plant in Brooklyn, Ohio. The Headliner closed in 1996. The days of hard drinking being mixed with news coverage are now long gone, and that's a good thing. But there are far fewer reporters out beating the bushes, and that's not a good thing.

AT LEAST THIS ONE WASN'T ON TV

This is likely my most embarrassing non-TV moment ever. I was at Channel 5 and reporter Dale Solly was at Channel 8. We became fast friends, working nights and showing up to cover many of the same stories. We later worked together at Channel 3. Eventually, he landed at a TV station in Washington, D.C.

No joke was too far out of bounds for Dale.

One of his cousins called me and told me that Dale was home from D.C. and that they and a couple of Dale's other cousins were going to be at the Headliner for a drink Friday night. I told him that I would come after the 11 p.m. news.

When I walked into the Headliner, it seemed like the perfect sit-uation for a surprise. The place was empty except the one booth where Dale and his cousins were sitting. Dale's back was to me. I don't know what came over me. I ran in, jumped on the booth seat behind him, and gave him a pretty good view of my private parts as he turned his head when hearing the noise behind him. It cracked everyone up. I got my cheap laugh. But months later it proved to have been an embarrassing decision.

I saw Dale's cousin a couple of times after that. "Dale always talks about what you did," he told me. "He thought it was hilarious." Such was our chop-busting relationship. Some months later, I got word that Dale had died in Washington after a jog. I attended the wake. There was a long line. When I got into the main room, I saw the family. One of the cousin's wives pointed in my direction. The cousin nodded yes. By her reaction, I knew she had asked about the

Headliner story and I was busted. That was awkward. It got worse.

Then I got to the casket. Knowing Dale, I expected him to sit up and say, "I got ya, you SOB!" He would do anything to "get you." I said a prayer and moved down the line to his mother. "Mrs. Solly, I'm so sorry," I said. "Dale and I had a lot of great times." "Yes," she answered. "I heard about the Headliner."

Once again, an embarrassing moment—and only myself to blame. That urge for attention always backfires on me!

NICE TRY

A man named Donato Lombardozzi had been convicted of murdering a co-worker at a pizza parlor. No one in the media knew anything about Lombardozzi or even had seen him. I had an idea. He was being held in the Cuyahoga County Jail pending his trial. *Why not go in and just sign in as a visitor and visit him?* I got lucky. Just ahead of me, a couple signed in to see him. I acted like I was there with them. This was good because I didn't have to sign my name and possibly tip off that I was with the media. We rode up the elevator to a visiting room. The others sat down with Lombardozzi and began to talk. I sat apart, trying to hear what was said. But not for long! After about two minutes, two jail security officers came into the room and began looking around. One pointed at me, the other nodded, and they gestured to me to come over to them. Busted! Someone had recognized me and told them to get me out of there. Nice guys, though; on the elevator all they said to me was, "Nice try." Lombardozzi was convicted and sentenced to life in prison.

GETTING YOUR ARMS AROUND A STORY

A doctor had been caught stealing drugs from his hospital by shortchanging patients in the operating room. Later, he had moved to another town and got his license back without any comment from the public or anyone else. I thought the public should know.

So I tracked him down. Cameraman John Potter recorded the whole thing. I saw a man using a leaf blower to clear the lawn at a large and beautiful home. He looked like the physician I remembered from the earlier stories. I went up and asked if he was the doctor I was looking for. He said no, but gave me a funny look. I took a chance. "Don't you remember me?" I asked. Then, he came at the camera and me, and we got into a kind of wrestling match right there on his lawn. As we grappled with one another, the doctor kept telling me to leave. I said, "Well, if we stop wrestling and let go of one another, that will happen." Eventually we both let go—and I had my story.

CHASING J. KEVIN KELLEY

J. Kevin Kelley worked in the Cuyahoga County Engineer's office. He was working to set up a new computer system. His real job was essentially being a fixer of sorts for County Commissioner Jimmy Dimora and County Auditor Frank Russo, both of whom wound up being convicted in the huge Cuyahoga County corruption scandal. Kelley would line up this or that deal and make connections for them.

He was the first person to "flip" during the FBI's investigation and tell the truth and implicate others. He did it on the first day they confronted him in the parking lot outside of the engineer's office. That fact is well known from trial testimony and federal filings.

He is the also the guy seen on a video clip often used on Channel 19 that shows his car, traveling at a high rate of speed, nearly hitting cameraman Marty DeChant.

After news of Kelley's involvement in the FBI investigation broke, he had been able to avoid reporters. We decided to park at the county engineer's office, located on the Superior Viaduct, and wait for him. Finally, we had spotted him leaving the building. We got out of our vehicle and started to approach him. He jumped in his car, hit the gas, and zoomed past, only an inch or two from

Marty. Gotta give Marty props; he nearly took one for the team that day!

What happened next has never been told. Marty and I were angry at the close call. We jumped in our news car and chased Kelley from the engineer's office down the Superior Viaduct and then onto West 25th Street. At some point Kelley caught a red light. We jumped out of our car—leaving it running in the middle of West 25th Street—and ran toward Kelley's car, but the light changed, and he sped off. Traffic was heavy, so we knew he couldn't get too far. We continued to chase him on foot for about a block. But he got away before we could ask a question.

As we walked back to our car, we were greeted—not too kindly— by drivers in the traffic we had blocked. Our car, still running, was in the middle of the street, both the driver's and passenger's doors still open. A few people laughed because they had seen the whole thing and knew we were a TV crew. The more frequent comment was, "A**holes, get out of the way."

Kelley entered a guilty plea and then went into hiding while he waited to be sentenced. After a long search, I learned he was at his mother's house in Florida. I told the news director that we needed to go and confront him, and he agreed. But I asked the news director not to say anything about the trip. There was a person in the newsroom whom I didn't trust. I knew this person had connections who would tip Kelley off about my going to Florida if word got out about it.

Marty and I went to Florida. On the first night there, we went to Kelley's mother's home after dark. There were voices in the fenced back yard. One sounded like Kelley, but I couldn't be sure. I tried to get video by holding a small camera over my head, but we had no luck. The next day we staked the place out, saw the same car that had nearly hit Marty a few months earlier, and followed it. We lost it in traffic. Back to the house. It was Halloween, and in late afternoon the kids were going door to door. As we watched, only Kelley's mother appeared at the door to hand out candy.

Our time was running out. We went to the door and rang the

bell. "Trick or Treat," I said, and then asked if Kevin was there. His mother explained that he was very sick and was in the hospital. We found no proof of that and never saw Kelley.

Back in Cleveland, we learned that by accident the news director had mentioned our Florida trip in the morning meeting, just as I had cautioned him not to do. It got back to me that the person I didn't trust had learned of our trip and had mentioned it to someone close to Kelley. We had been doomed from the start!

Weeks later I saw Kelley's attorney at the courthouse. "Trick or treat," he said. "Very funny." He smiled, but I don't think he really thought it was too funny.

After missing Kelley in Florida, I got a second chance some months later when I heard that he was returning to Cleveland for a court hearing. I was able to find out what flight he was on. That night when he arrived at Hopkins Airport, he finally had to face the camera. He didn't say much, but it made me feel better.

I DIDN'T THINK IT WAS VERY FUNNY

I once thought I was going to be in a helicopter crash. We had flown to Ashtabula to report on a long strike by the nurses at a hospital. On the way back to Cleveland, the pilot let me fly the chopper. The dual controls were in the cockpit because he had been training someone that day. The pilot was an instructor, so there was nothing wrong with what we were doing.

What I didn't know was that the pilot and the cameraman, who was in the back seat, hatched a plan over the headset that I couldn't hear. The pilot vectored me over the cooling stacks at the Eastlake power plant. I don't understand all the avionics of it, but he knew that by doing this the chopper would fall some distance due to the heat discharge from the smokestacks. He was right. I was at the controls and down the thing went. It stayed level but it fell a good bit. I almost fainted (among other bodily functions) until I heard the two of them laugh hysterically. I didn't think it was too funny at the time.

GETTING PUSHED AROUND

IN THE COURSE OF DOING my job, I ruffled more than a few feathers. Sometimes, people I reported on tried to get back at me. In another chapter, I have already talked about police officers putting me on the NCIC fugitive from justice most-wanted list. Other examples are far more local, and usually far more physical or embarrassing in nature. That was part of the job. And to be honest, I loved when it happened. It gave me that news rush that I lived for. When someone reacts to you with violence it does two things. First, it shows that they've got something to hide. Second, it makes a memorable, visual moment—and TV news stories are all about memorable, visual moments.

THE SKIN GAME

It's probably an exaggeration to say that this story is about getting pushed around. However, it is an example of a business trying to get back at me for catching them doing something they shouldn't have been doing. All these years later it is funny, but at the time I felt the repercussions.

The owner of this business came up with a unique, nonviolent way to pay me back for reporting on the business in a news story.

Brookpark Road in parts of Brook Park and Cleveland was a strip of "adult entertainment" joints and low-cost motels. Tom Coyne, the long-time mayor of Brook Park, had for many years waged a war on those businesses. To his credit, he eventually won that war. His officers busted many dirty bookstores and movie houses with dark booths where anonymous sexual encounters were going on. The story I reported had a different focus, though. It had to do with racial discrimination.

I had received several tips that one of the strip clubs was discriminating against Black patrons, even to the point of denying them admittance. I set up a sting. A strip club on Brookpark Road was not news. Discrimination by a licensed business would be, though. And the fact that the discrimination was alleged to happen at a strip club—well, that made it an easy sell to station managers for the upcoming ratings period. We came up with a great title: "The Skin Game."

I arranged for six men—three white guys and three Black guys—to help with the sting. They would dress identically and then, separately, go to the club. The white guys had no problems. The went in, got drinks, and had dances done for them, for a fee. All legal.

The Black guys (remember, dressed identically to the white guys) got to the door and the doorman said, "Oh, sorry—gotta be wearing a shirt with a collar" or "Sorry buddy, no hoodies allowed" or "No hats allowed." Then, one by one, they changed what they were wearing in the parking lot, waited a while, and returned to the doorman. Grudgingly, they were allowed in.

I had wireless microphones on each set of guys so that what happened at the door and then inside was recorded. The Black men sat at the bar and were ignored. One said, "Hey, can I get a drink?" He was ignored. He asked again. The barmaid came over and said, "I'm sorry, I can't serve you a drink or I'll be in trouble." Another asked a dancer nearby, "Can we get a dance?" She said, "I can't dance for you or I'll get fired." It went on and on.

Later, I tried to enter the club with my cameraman and was stopped at the door by an off-duty suburban police officer working security. Nothing happened, as the owner wasn't there. I got a compelling, ratings-grabbing story out of my sting.

What happened next was both interesting, and embarrassing.

After the story aired, the strip club was denied a renewal of its liquor license by the State of Ohio. The owner was no dummy. He fought back. He reopened the club as an all-nude "juice bar." That was legal in Ohio because no alcohol was served. Next came the payback to me.

It actually began even before he lost his liquor license. He put one of those large, mobile signs out in front of the bar with a message reading, "Rated Number One by Paul Orlousky and TV 3." A later version, which I didn't see myself but was told about, read, "Thanks Paul O, the man who brought nudity to Brook Park."

OK, I'm a big boy, I can take it. The problem was that after the signs appeared, I started getting phone calls from people saying that they couldn't believe I would endorse such a place. I tried to explain that it was just a payback for a critical story I had done. The response was always the same: "Don't make excuses. You should be ashamed of yourself," followed by a click. There wasn't much we could do—until the club's owner ran radio commercials delivering the same message. That is when the station's legal department got involved, and the campaign ended.

I saved one letter the station received, from a woman who wrote, "If Paul Orlousky has nothing better to report on than 'The Skin Game,' perhaps he should sweep the floors at Channel 3 and at the same time clean up his reporting."

She's welcome to her opinion about my reporting, but remember: It was a story about overt racial discrimination. I couldn't help where it was happening. If it happened at a church and I did the story, would it have made any difference? Plain Dealer reporter and TV critic Tom Feran ran a story in which he quoted me saying, "It happened at a trashy place, I hope it wasn't a trashy story." Feran called it the most substantive piece any station had done during the ratings sweeps. Not everyone agreed.

A couple of days after the story aired came a predictable letter from a large law firm representing the bar, threatening me with a lawsuit and demanding that we keep all our recordings. Nothing came of it except that six months later the club entered a guilty plea on a discrimination charge. Oh, there was another good reason why the lawsuit wasn't pursued. What the club owner and lawyers didn't know was that all six men who helped with the sting, both Black and white, were Cleveland Police officers. A pretty solid group.

Still, the club owner couldn't let it rest. Some time later, I received a T-shirt from him in the mail with letters written in silver glitter, "To Paul O., the man whose stories brought nudity to Brook Park. Thanks." I still have the shirt, as well as a photo of the sign that the owner sent me a couple of years ago. Although my story got him, he knows he got me at least a little, and he enjoyed that.

"WE'D ALL LIKE TO BAN PAUL ORLOUSKY"

Another story from Brookpark Road comes to mind. The owner of a closed-down motel had been cited for what the City of Brook Park deemed a dangerous situation that wasn't being remedied at his property. At issue was an abandoned swimming pool filled with filthy water and debris from a fallen ceiling—along with other smelly stuff. The fear was that someone could fall into it and drown if the situation weren't abated by draining it or properly cordoning it off.

I went to the site with cameraman Kevin Dorenkott to see if what I had been told was true. It was. Midway through our filming, a man who said he was the owner approached us and told us to get out. We immediately began to retreat. As we did, Kevin kept the video rolling as we backpedaled away from the guy down a couple of hallways and around corners. "Why are you still rolling?" the owner asked. I said, "To document that we are doing exactly what you are asking us to do. Leaving." It was the perfect way to prevent him from later saying we ignored his demand. We left, and I thought that was the end of it.

Later that afternoon there was a court hearing regarding the city's effort to force the owner to make the property safe. I had cameraman Gary Graves attend. I didn't attend personally because I didn't expect much to happen. I was back at WOIO preparing my story. Gary returned from court. "Orlo, you won't believe what happened," he said. He cued up the tape and I watched, amused by what I saw.

The owner of the motel was more concerned with his confrontation with us that afternoon than actually doing anything about correcting his pool problem. Although it was off-topic for the court proceedings, he railed to the judge that he objected to our confronting him. Judge Timothy McGinty, a former assistant county prosecutor with a well-developed sense of humor, took it all in. He and I had conflicts in the past, but I considered him a good guy and family man, and still do.

McGinty saw an opening. With a large smirk on his face, he said to the property owner, "It sounds to me like you are asking me to ban Paul Orlousky. I can't do that." Then, looking squarely at the camera, and with a larger smile and knowing that I would see it later, he said, "We've all wanted to ban Paul Orlousky at one time or another; but I can't do that. It's not something I can do."

McGinty later became an aggressive and, I believe, effective Cuyahoga County prosecutor. He never stopped ruffling feathers. Not everyone took it as a badge of honor as I did, though. His honest but confrontational style angered some people, including some in his voter base of the Cleveland West Side Irish community, an important political force. After two terms he was defeated.

HATE MAIL FROM A MAIL CARRIER

I've received a good bit of hate mail over my career, but the most unusual letter came from a United States Postal Service mail carrier. It was delivered to my home, in our curbside mailbox, by a carrier in one of the typical USPS delivery trucks. I do not know if it was my carrier, but we saw the truck arrive, went out and got the mail, and found only one letter. It was stamped but not cancelled, which made it untraceable to a particular post office. I quickly learned why. The letter was an angry response to a story I had done about the mail delivery on my street. Whoever left it knew what he or she was doing. My regular delivery of mail came later that day. Something was fishy.

The background: There had been a bad snowstorm a few days before Christmas in 2004. Our street was slushy and unplowed. That night the temperature plunged, and the street became a sheet of ice. And not smooth ice. Deep ruts had been left by cars' tires in the slush before it all froze.

The Post Office decided to suspend deliveries on the street. The problem was that it was a few days before Christmas and there were many kids on the street expecting gifts from out of town relatives. Those gifts didn't arrive in time for Christmas. This was odd, because I noticed that each day delivery trucks from private companies had no problems navigating the street. *Time to get to the bottom of this*, I thought.

Cameraman Kevin Dorenkott and I shot video on the street a couple of days after Christmas. Postal deliveries were still not being made. We showed that it didn't take much effort to simply lean out of the truck a foot or so and make the deliveries to the curbside mailboxes. I left a message with the US Postal Service requesting an explanation. We headed back to the station, but on the way, we saw something interesting: At a shopping plaza not far from my house, three postal trucks were parked at a sandwich shop. The carriers were inside at a table talking. Meanwhile, other delivery companies continued to crisscross the city making deliveries, including to merchants at the plaza. It made for great video.

It was not a major investigation. Still, no mail for five days seemed ridiculous. The postal service called me back, and I set up an interview. At the main branch downtown, I asked the spokesman about the issue. His reply made the story even better. "Well," he said, "you know the customer always has the option of going to their branch to pick up the mail at the end of the day after the carrier has returned." I couldn't resist pointing out the obvious: "But if the customer can get to the post office, why can't the post office get to the customer?" He said something about safety concerns.

Back to the hate mail. The writer went on and on about the dedicated people who deliver, sort, and handle mail. I have no doubt they're dedicated. Yet there was one mistake in the letter, a quote that is wrongly cited as the post office's motto: "Neither snow nor rain nor heat nor gloom of night stays these couriers from the swift completion of their appointed rounds." The USPS spokesperson that day educated me, saying it didn't apply to them because that motto is only above the doors of the main post offices in New York City and Washington, DC—it is not the motto of the United States Postal Service. Certainly in this story "the swift completion of their appointed rounds" didn't apply.

REALLY GETTING PUSHED AROUND

When I was assigned to cover a story on a certain street or in a certain area, sometimes I'd think *Here we go . . .* I just knew there was gonna be trouble. There were many. When I hear East 131st Street, East 93rd Street, Morris Black Place, West 80th Street at Madison Avenue and many others I still get that feeling. But two streets, both running off West 65th Street just north of Lorain Avenue and I-90, take the cake.

I've probably had a dozen or so serious physical altercations of having to fight someone off or keep them from attacking the cameraman over the years. Of that number, I bet half were either on Lawn Avenue or Colgate Avenue (and the adjacent and even worse Colgate Court, where the homes look like garages).

As soon as we showed up on those streets at a location where something bad had happened, we were confronted by, *"Get the f*** outta here!"* Usually spoken by a big brute with a beard who smelled like he had been drinking.

Young reporters reading this, take note. You can get through such threatening behavior, but you must know what to do. First, the brute confronting you often has only one eye looking at you. The other is off at an angle. This can be a problem for you if you don't pick one eye and stick with it. If you switch eyes, they think you are dissing them, and trouble will follow. Next, you will be asked the question, "You think you are better than me, don't you?" There is no correct answer.

Think about it. If you say no, you are empowering someone who is about to attack you. It makes you seem weak. If you say yes, you appear to think you are better than they are. You are also likely to be attacked no matter what you say, so keep your distance. The shotgun microphone, which can record from farther away, will get all the audio you need.

I learned this the hard way one night when a guy fitting the description above came at cameraman Pete Miller and me, swinging wildly at the camera. We were doing a follow-up story about his pit bull attacking and mauling a small child. That night, Pete was using a monopod to steady his camera. It is basically just an expandable piece of metal from the ground to his camera. At one point the attacker grabbed the monopod. I tried to stop him, and it broke loose from the camera and now he and I were in a tug of war with the thing. Then, he let go and I had the monopod in my hand and was using it like a baseball bat, warning him to stay away.

There is a better solution. Go to the scene while the police are still there. If the assignment desk tells you to go there after dark, ask the person sending you there to come along. Same goes for assignments to go and question the family of a murder victim. Just say, "Great idea, this would be good cross-training for you."

WHAT IF I AM?

One confrontation I had early in my time in Cleveland taught me a lot about how to read people.

Police had busted a hydroponic marijuana-growing operation in an old factory in the Collinwood neighborhood of Cleveland. We toured the setup with police and got the soundbites and video we needed for the early news. From a police source, I found out where the suspect who had been arrested lived. The source told me the suspect had bonded out and might already be home.

Cameraman Tom Livingston and I went to the suspect's house and were greeted by a young man on the porch who was hysterical, waving his arms wildly and yelling "Why are you here? What do you want?" Clearly, he knew why we were there and was upset at the arrest of a family member. We kept our distance because of his demeanor. Someone in the home made a phone call to the suspect we were looking for, because almost immediately we heard screeching car tires coming around the corner. It was one of those huge cars from the late 1970s just like in *Goodfellas* or *Kill the Irishman*.

One Hispanic man got out of the car, still holding a mixed drink from a nearby bar, and began yelling at us. Then, a big Italian-looking fella got out and told us to go away. We were on the sidewalk, so we were OK legally, but he was a big man, and it seemed like he had been drinking, too.

"Get out!" he said. We held our ground.

"We're just looking for Jim," I said.

"Jim ain't here, OK?"

Over the years, I had learned how to read people. The way he said "OK" was a challenge, like *What are you gonna do about it?* And it told me that I was talking to Jim.

"Are you Jim?" I asked.

"Yeah, what if I am?" he snapped back. The "What if I am" part told me he wasn't going to back down. He had a tough guy image to maintain in his neighborhood.

I told him I just wanted to hear what he had to say.

"Nothing."

You need to know when to leave, and it was now. We left. But the confrontation had just made my story more compelling!

TAKE THAT CAMERA AND SHOVE IT

A cameraman I worked with at WKYC, Ed Verba, had been around town for many years. He had two catch phrases. When a new reporter would ask him to speed or go through a red light to get to a fire he'd say, "Hey, if this fire is good enough to be on the news at 6 o'clock, it will still be burning when we get there." The other was, "I don't learn any new reporter's name for at least a year because most don't last that long. You know in thirty years that's probably a couple hundred names I didn't have to remember."

One day out on a story Ed came up with another insightful quote. A builder had put up a house for a suburban police officer and done a bad job. It was horrible. We went to take a look at it and saw frost forming in the corners of the living room. When we walked down the steps, the ceiling above us didn't match the angle of the steps. As we came down toward the bottom step, we almost had to tilt our heads to the side so that we didn't hit our heads on the ceiling above. There were many other problems. We talked to the officer and his wife, and then went on a search for the builder. We found him on a different job site in a different city.

His father was helping him and saw us arrive and get out of the news car with the camera. He ran to his pickup truck, and as we approached the site he pulled his truck between us and the job site, blocking us from crossing the street. Ed and I would move to our right and he would back up to the right, blocking us. We would go to the left and he would pull forward, blocking our shot. This dance continued for about a minute. It was awkward because he was in the driver's seat only about three feet from me.

He had run to the truck and was breathing heavily. "You look kinda winded," I said. "Is that camera on?" he asked. I said it was. He replied, "Take that camera and shove it up your ass." I told him I wasn't gonna do that. "Is that microphone on?" he asked. I told him it was. He replied, "Take that and shove it up your ass, too." The microphone was still attached to the camera, so I grabbed it and moved it closer to him saying. "I don't think I got all of that," I told him. He reached out and took a big slap at the microphone, knocking it out of my hand. Because of his diversion, his son was able to get into the passenger side of his truck. Then, they sped away. Ed continued to roll tape. Eventually, he stopped rolling. "Orlo," he said, "this was a good story, but he just made it a way better story than it really is."

QUESTION BETTER NOT ASKED

When I give a speech or make a public appearance, I will often be asked about some of my confrontations. "Aren't you worried about it when they attack?" someone will ask. I'll answer, "No, they always go after the camera first." It gets a laugh, but really it's important to know that the camera blocks the entire field of view for the cameraperson on the right side. The reporter must be aware of that—and be ready to step in when necessary.

Cameraman Marty DeChant and I, after nearly twenty years of working together almost every day, were particularly good at anticipating each other's moves. One day, we went to Elyria to report on an incident in which a man bought a gun and then immediately went to his wife's place of business and shot her dead. First we got the basics at the scene of the shooting. Then we went to the gun store to see if they could tell us anything. I had a pleasant conversation with a clerk behind the counter and asked if the owner was there. The clerk said no. I gave him a business card with my phone number on it.

When we had walked into the store, a second man in the middle of the store had been acting kind of sheepish. I figured he was probably the owner but couldn't be sure. That is, until I was handing the business card to the clerk. Then, I heard noise behind me and turned. The sheepish guy, who we later learned was indeed the owner, had begun pushing Marty around. With a heavy camera on his shoulder, it is especially dangerous for a cameraman to be pushed around. I ran to his aid and got between them. We were close to the door and the store owner pushed us out. Marty managed to get it all on camera. I kept my body between the owner and the open door so he couldn't close it and asked a couple of questions. It got a little rough as he pushed me to try to get to the door handle. At that point I was agitated, so I yelled my final question at him, "Who do you think you're dealing with, some kind of an idiot?" Loaded question. Luckily, all he said was, "Get out!" and slammed the door. He missed the obvious comeback answer to my question!

DUCKING CHERRY BOMBS AT THE STADIUM

Another example of cameraman danger came at the final Cleveland Browns game at Municipal Stadium on December 17, 1995, not long after Art Modell had announced he was moving the team to Baltimore. The crowd was in a foul mood. Many of the scoreboard advertisers had had their signs removed or obscured. Cameraman George Payamgis and I were on the field. As the game wound down, fans began to throw firecrackers onto the field. Not small ones, either—big ones like ash cans and cherry bombs. My job was to watch for incoming explosives as George tried to shoot the action on the field. "On your right, George," I'd say, and he'd scurry left to dodge the explosion. It happened over and over. No one was trying to throw them at us—they were just throwing them. No small amount of beer had been guzzled by the crowd that afternoon, which didn't help matters. It was a dangerous place for us to be.

We were at the Dawg Pound end of the stadium, where the seats were very close to the field. The game officials wisely decided to move the action to the other end of the field, where the stands were much farther from the players.

When the game ended, Browns players came to the Dawg Pound end of the field slapping high fives with the fans, hugging some and saying thank you. The fireworks stopped. For a few minutes.

After the players left the field, a different kind of barrage began. Huge pieces of the bleachers in the Dawg Pound were ripped from their foundations and thrown onto the field. In other areas of the stadium, fans set fire to whatever wood they could find. The police were outnumbered and could do nothing. It was surreal!

We left the field and went outside and saw fans carrying large sections of seats up West Third Street, four and five at a time, still bolted together as they had been in the stands.

It was a sad end to decades of great memories at Municipal Stadium.

SPAT ON

As should be abundantly clear by now, when you report TV news stories that piss people off, those people sometimes piss back. Or, as in this case, they spit. Enter a notorious family from Cleveland's West Side.

I had done stories about a family that had set up a charity claiming to share its phone solicitation proceeds with the needy. The problem was, as I had been told, they didn't share very much. It was basically just a phone bank to solicit donations. I don't think they were getting rich, but they weren't delivering what they claimed.

I had obtained some of their financial records. I had to get someone inside the charity to learn more. One of the charity's claims was that they hired and trained homeless people and others in need of help. To check, I had one of our interns go and apply for a job. She was a college graduate, well spoken, well dressed and clearly not in need of a handout. She was offered a job instantly. She never took the job; but it proved the claim that it was not a homeless training program.

The story aired, and the family didn't like it one bit. My phone rang at all times of the day and night. My voice mail was completely full every day when I got to work. Unsigned threatening letters came in the mail. On and on it went. They even displayed three-by-four-foot posters of me in each of their office windows. These were not flattering images; they showed me as Mickey Mouse wearing a pointed dunce hat, holding a station microphone, with my name on the hat and the word "Duh" coming out of my mouth.

I thought it creative but not the best public relations. What should I do? I called the owner one day and I asked him if I could get a copy of one of the posters because I liked them. He swore at me and hung up. The posters were gone the next day. I sure wish I had gotten ahold of one or had at least taken a photo.

It didn't end there. A Cleveland police detective called me and asked if we could meet. I thought maybe he would be able to get me some relief from this harassment. We met in a conference room at the TV station. He took out a notebook and made notes in it as we talked. The questioning continued, and suddenly I could see where it was going. "Are you asking me if I ever bribed anyone for their financial records?" I asked him. He said yes, that's what he was asking. "Absolutely not," I replied. He shut his notebook and left. It turned out that the family had made a bribery claim against me just to further harass me.

My story had gotten the FBI involved, and they launched an investigation. I knew nothing of it at the time, but eventually the charity was indicted and one of the family members running it was sentenced to prison.

On the day he was to be sentenced, I was waiting outside the federal courthouse in Cleveland. I knew he was going to prison and wanted to get a comment from his brother, who was also involved in the charity but had not been charged. The brother came around the corner near the federal courthouse and I asked for a comment. "Mr. Orlousky," he said, "go and f*** yourself." I asked another question, and he said the same thing. We continued up the steps and as he got to the door, I asked him if he had brought a tooth-brush for his brother. He said, "No," then turned, quickly drawing a deep breath, and lurched forward and spat in my face.

I turned my head quickly, and he only got me on the cheek. The mix of coffee and cigarettes in his saliva was no fun to be around. I headed home, showered, and took my clothes to the dry cleaner. Not a great beginning to a day.

There was another part of the story that I was unaware of at the time.

It seems that at some point, in the middle of the night, the owner called the FBI office and left a message for the special agent in charge: "One of these days you're going to wind up at the end of a rope." That got the owner about three and a half years in prison.

The special agent in charge and I were friendly because our kids had attended college together. When I saw him later at a gathering of some sort, I had to ask: "He called me for months, hundreds and maybe thousands of times. Tied up all my communication. He calls you once, and gets three and a half years in prison?" I mentioned that I had reached out to the police, the FBI, and other agencies, yet nothing happened. He got a broad smile on his face and said, "Paul, that tells me one thing." I asked what. "Clearly we're on different levels of the food chain," he said. We had a hearty laugh!

HORRIFIC STORIES

THE FIRST FATAL ACCIDENT

Over the years I have been to dozens of shootings, fatal car crashes, and fires. I don't feel the need to recount the horrors of watching a shooting victim die in front of your eyes, or of bodies being taken from burning buildings or extracted from mangled cars. But something I was told a long time ago has proved true: You never forget your first fatality.

I was probably only about seventeen or eighteen and doing weekend news on WENY Radio in Elmira, New York. I heard a call over the police scanner about a boy on a bicycle who had been hit by a car on Route 17 in the nearby town of Big Flats. I got a 16-millimeter film camera and headed to the scene.

As I got out of my car at the accident, I saw a twisted bicycle and a car with a large dent in the front hood and grill. I began to take some footage. Then I got closer, and I saw a tarp covering a small form. It was the boy who had been riding the bicycle. I had never seen anything like this before. But that wasn't the most gripping thing I saw. There, next to the tarp, was a half-melted ice cream cone. The boy had crossed the highway to an ice cream stand on the other side. While crossing back to his home he had been struck and killed. The ice cream cone lasted longer than he did. What a sad image.

To this day I have a vision of that kid, excited to have ice cream and probably not paying attention, being hit and killed.

ARIEL CASTRO

Some stories I covered were eye opening and jaw dropping. Occasionally across the nation. One of those was a story I broke.

I had just gotten home from work and it was about six o'clock in the evening. I had been on the 5 p.m. news for a story that I don't remember now. I do remember what happened next. At about ten minutes after six I got a call from a trusted source who said, "They just found those missing girls." I asked if it was Amanda Berry and Gina DeJesus. I had covered their unexplained and unsolved disappearances for nearly a decade. He said, "Yes, and a third girl." I was stunned and said, "Another body?" I assumed that after all the years they were dead. He said, "No, alive!" I told him that I'd call him right back and ran to my garage.

I jumped in the car and drove back toward downtown like a madman. I called the station news director, Dan Salamone. He always trusted me. I told him to get every resource we had to Seymour Avenue on Cleveland's near West Side. He never hesitated, even when I told him the almost unimaginable news: They were alive!

I called my source back to get all the details. Turns out, I got the tip only about six minutes after the rescue of the three women. We got on the air immediately, with me filling in the details I obtained with my cell phone while racing east on I-90. We beat the other stations by forty or forty-five minutes because they couldn't confirm the information I had. When I got to Seymour Avenue, where the girls had been held captive, my fellow Channel 19 reporter Tiffani Tucker was already on the air live from the scene. There was a celebratory atmosphere there. Neighbors were joyous that the girls—now women—had been found. That emotion was mixed with disbelief that they had been held in a home so nearby for so long, undetected.

I filled in what I knew; and we were on the air nonstop until about 1 or 2 a.m.

It was a blur! I did live hits for Anderson Cooper and CNN, and many other shows—including my station, obviously. One blended into the next. I went home and slept for about three hours, and we were back on the air before dawn. The next day the network demands came from CBS, CNN, the BBC, Japan, Finland, and many more. You name it, we did it. It remains a foggy memory for me because it happened so fast.

Ariel Castro had been arrested almost immediately. He was at a fast-food spot nearby getting food for his captives. Amanda Berry had been able to get the attention of a passerby, which triggered the rescue. The women told the passerby where Castro was, and then the Cleveland Police rounded him up. He entered a guilty plea and was sentenced to life in prison. About a month later, he hanged himself in prison. He died a coward. He spent less than one percent of the time behind bars that he had held his victims captive in his self-fashioned prison.

ANTHONY SOWELL

I don't know what to say about Anthony Sowell. He seduced women with drugs, had sex with them, then attacked and murdered eleven of them. Making it more macabre was the fact that he either buried them in his house or back yard, or just put their bodies in closets to decompose.

The day he walked into court for his arraignment was very strange. I was there to cover the story, and I found myself standing close to a guy who would later be proven to have murdered eleven people. I just stared at him trying to comprehend the situation. I never did really wrap my mind around it. He was eventually found guilty and sentenced to life in prison.

Gruesome details of the story have been well documented elsewhere. I reported from the scene in disbelief as body after body was brought out. The story about Anthony Sowell haunts me.

A related story came out a few days after the news broke, and I feel better about that one. A family-run meat processing company, Ray's Sausage, a minority-owned business, was located next door to Sowell's home on Imperial Avenue. Before the bodies were discovered there had been complaints about bad odors in the neighborhood. The city's first target was Ray's. The owner was forced to make what turned out to be unnecessary sewer repairs and other changes. Tens of thousands of dollars were spent by Ray's—a big expense for a small business.

While Ray's suffered undue damage, the city apparently ignored the fact that there had been numerous reports of many women missing in that neighborhood. One woman who had escaped Sowell's home had even made a police report. Yet instead of running down those leads, the city focused on Ray's, an easy target. Of course, after the bodies were found it was clear what the problem had been all along.

I did a couple of stories about the fact that the city, in the days after the discovery of the bodies, had promised to make Ray's whole. The city never did. However, Ray's daughter, after getting some advice from a financial advisor who had seen their plight on television, put every dime she had into rebuilding the business. She told me recently that they now sell Ray's Sausage in three states. I have seen how it is produced, in a kitchen as sanitary as you could ever imagine.

LUNDGREN CULT KILLINGS

Jeffrey Lundgren, a religious leader who had set up a cult in Kirtland, Ohio, became a shocking figure in the news the day he led the Avery family—a father, mother, and their three children—into a barn at the back of his property, had them stand over graves that he had dug, and shot them one by one. He felt they were straying from his teachings.

I was on the scene the night the whole thing was discovered. It was chilling as an ambulance with the bodies of five innocent victims drove past us. And it was just as chilling later when Lundgren was led past me at the Lake County Sheriff's office. He had dead eyes. Eyes that send a chill down your spine when they meet yours. People can talk about a chilling interaction; this was more than that. I felt like the air temperature dropped fifteen degrees when he looked at me. I may have seen the devil. That devil was executed by lethal injection years later. I was outside the prison when the hearse carrying him out passed by. Certainly not the same feeling as when the ambulance with those bodies went past.

Many years later, Marty and I were on another story and drove by the Lundgren property. We stopped and walked into the barn. The unearthed graves were still there, filled with water. There were bullet holes in one of the walls. I don't know why I wanted to go back. It was a dark place, but not compared to the darkness I saw in Lundgren's eyes.

TENAI MOORE

This is a horrible story, but one that taught me a lot. A 3-year-old girl named Tenai Moore had drowned at the Cleveland Heights YMCA. I covered the story for the early news that day. Then, it was time for me to see if the family wanted to speak to us for the later newscasts. This is always the worst of the worst assignments. Mr. Moore, Tenai's father, taught me a lesson that day.

I walked toward the door of the family's home, and before I got there a man with eyes swollen from crying came around the corner of the house. "You must be Mr. Moore," I said. "Yes, I am," he replied. I introduced myself and apologized for being there. I told him that there was no camera rolling but I just wanted to see if he had a nice picture of his daughter, or if there was anything he wanted us to share. He said, "I know who you are, Paul. She was a nice little girl. I'd like to talk about her."

This experience reinforced something I have always practiced: Never to walk up to any victim with a camera. Sometimes they respond like Mr. Moore, but other times they say, "How could you come to my door at a time like this?" That is when I say, "That is why the camera and the microphone are in the car. I'm sorry to bother you." Many times, they appreciate that we were not in their face and share a picture for us to use or an off-camera tribute. These situations are the worst part of being a news reporter.

CLOVERLEAF SPEEDWAY

On a Sunday night in July 1982, we heard on a police scanner that there had been a serious accident at Cloverleaf Speedway in Valley View. A car making a turn on the oval track started to roll over. As it did, the housing around the transmission exploded, sending a piece of metal into the stands that hit a young girl and killed her.

We went to the hospital, and at some point the family came out. Another TV station was there and approached them. They got nothing. I stayed back and did not approach. Later, a letter came to the station. It was from the mother of that little girl. Her name was Mrs. Pam Petersen. She noticed that I had been there at the hospital and respected her family's privacy at such a terrible moment. She wrote that she would never watch another station because of how I handled the situation. In fact, she also called us in the days later and asked for help in notifying family members who were on an Alaskan cruise and hadn't heard of the death. Over the years, I got some compelling stories from people to whom she gave my name. She told them about her experience with me. This might be a lesson for young reporters: Treat people the way you want to be treated. It will pay dividends over the long haul.

I kept her letter, either in my desk or on my desk, until the day I retired. I still have it in front of me as I write this. It grounds me. Sometimes, when I got too aggressive, reading it reminded me to keep myself in check. She did me a great service in what would be any parent's worst of times.

SHOOTING AT CWRU

Our assignment desk heard on police scanners that there was an urgent call for "all hands-on deck" to get to the campus of

Case Western Reserve University. A graduate student, Biswanath Halder, had entered the building carrying a semi-automatic rifle and wearing a flak jacket. He was roaming the halls while randomly shooting. We learned later that Halder was upset about one of his dissertations being rejected by the faculty.

Cameraman Gary Graves and I got there quickly. So quickly that we were already inside the perimeter the police set up to keep people away from danger. We were closer even than most of the officers who responded. This was an active shooter situation, and we were dangerously close to the building. We were in a live-broadcast truck, though, which gave us a little protection. I had Gary set up a signal back to the station as soon as it got dark. It would have been foolish to do it during daylight because we would be seen. This way we didn't have to move around and become possible targets. We hid behind a large tree in case there was more shooting. Roughly one hundred people were being held hostage or were hiding in their offices.

Negotiations with SWAT weren't making any progress. Fortunately, most of the trapped people who had barricaded themselves in offices had access to telephones. Over the seven-hour standoff, police pinpointed where each of them was located and devised a plan on how to get them out safely. The building where this happened had an unusual design that included no long hallways. This provided Halder with many places to fire from. But police had an ingenious plan. When they encountered Halder, they drove him higher in the building, floor by floor. Because of this strategy, those trapped on lower floors could escape.

Shuttle buses were brought in, guarded by SWAT officers with machine guns and even a tank. These went to a side door. A dozen or so hostages scurried onto a bus, which then drove off. Then another bus arrived and another dozen people were safe.

Because of our location, Gary and I were able to broadcast the entire rescue drama live on the air. All the other stations were outside the perimeter more than a block away. Eventually it seemed that everyone was safe. SWAT went in and got Halder.

Sadly, they found something else: the body of graduate student Norman Wallace and two wounded professors who survived.

Halder is serving life in prison.

CHARDON HIGH SCHOOL

The murders of innocent students at Chardon High School on February 27, 2012 shocked the nation. Among the first to learn of them that morning was Julia Tullos on the WOIO assignment desk, who heard on a police radio scanner the huge dispatch of officers from many communities to Chardon. We rushed to Chardon to cover the story.

Marty and I were in Akron, just about to enter the federal courthouse to cover the Jimmy Dimora trial in the Cuyahoga County corruption scandal. We quickly sped north. Marty used an app on his phone to listen to police radio calls from the Chardon area. I listened to his phone with one ear; in the other ear I had my phone, with which I could go on the air and also listen to the station's live feed so that I could be ready when they came to me. Marty was also using a third phone to talk to Julia and get any information she had learned. It was a hectic ride.

As we drove up the hill on Route 44 into Chardon, it hit both of us. We looked to the right at a shopping plaza parking lot. There were medical helicopters there. The blades weren't spinning. It was clear they weren't in a rush. That told us that there were likely fatalities. The next thing we saw was a gurney being wheeled slowly toward one of the helicopters. Safety force officers used a sheet to protect the identity of the dead person. We knew it was bad.

Arriving at the high school, we saw that students had been evacuated and were only being released when a parent or guardian came to get them. It was in some ways chaotic, but in other ways showed that the planning for such an incident had helped those parents whose children were not injured learn that their child was safe.

We eventually learned that a student named T.J. Lane had been sitting at a cafeteria table, waiting for a bus ride to a vocational school for class, when he suddenly leapt to his feet and began firing. Some of his victims were targets, others just in the wrong place at the wrong time. In all six students were hit by his gunfire. Three died. One is confined to a wheelchair.

The days following the shooting were difficult. And months later, I saw the most despicable act I have ever witnessed in my life.

Lane pleaded guilty. At his sentencing, security was tight. The families were seated in the audience. Reporters and cameras were in the jury box. As the hearing proceeded, Lane appeared to be doing something with his shirt. I didn't think much of it. He'd undo one button, then after a minute or two another. Certainly, the judge and attorneys who were busy with their work didn't notice. When it came time for Lane to speak, he stood up, opened his shirt, and turned to the families. Scrawled on his undershirt was the word "killer." That was horrible, but it got worse.

Next, Lane addressed the families saying. "The hand that pulled the trigger that killed your sons now masturbates to the memory." he said. "F*** you all." There were gasps and some began to cry.

I always thought there was no way you could inflict additional pain on the parent of a murdered child. I was wrong. I now know that there is a special place in hell for certain people.

RESPECTING PEOPLE

A plane crashed in Amish country in a rural county, and I was sent on the station's helicopter to report on it. We found the wreckage and got footage from the air; then it was time to land. I didn't want to offend the Amish residents, who generally shun modern conveniences like electricity and certainly helicopters, by landing one on their property. So we circled until I spotted a nearby home that had electric wires leading to it. This clearly was not an Amish home. The pilot landed with no problem or objection.

An Amish man who had witnessed the crash said he appreciated that we hadn't invaded his property or trampled on his beliefs. Surprisingly, he agreed to an on-camera interview—with the stipulation that we shoot it from behind him, not showing his face. Had we landed on his property, I'm sure he never would have talked to us.

Sadly, the video we got on the ground showed the plane being turned over to reveal six dead passengers.

THE RAVENNA BABY MURDER

This story made national news. A woman who couldn't have children befriended a pregnant woman at a Walmart in Ravenna. One day, she invited the pregnant woman to her home, killed her, and cut the nearly full-term baby from her womb.

Before all the sensational details were known, a local search began for the missing mom. Then it became a regional search. I was in Ravenna every night. No sign of her. After about four or five days, we didn't know if it made any sense to keep returning to Ravenna, because there was nothing new to report. At the afternoon meeting, I said, "Well, if something does happen, we are about fifty minutes away and won't get much of anything." We went back to Ravenna, and once again found nothing was happening. Cameraman Dan "Wags" Wagner and I were in the news van at the police parking lot. He was editing what little new video we had. At the same time, I watched to see if anything happened. Suddenly, Ravenna Police cars, Portage County Sheriff's cars, and Ohio Highway Patrol cars all began to pull out one by one. We decided to follow.

We arrived at a location we hadn't been to in the previous days. The law enforcement vehicles we had seen pull out of the police parking lot were now backed into several driveways. No sirens had been used, and their lights were off. It was ominous.

From experience I knew they were staging for some kind of operation. I said to Wags, "We better get outta here, something is about to happen." I didn't want us to be in the way of law enforcement. As we drove past quickly, we saw some action begin behind us. I believe I heard a gunshot. Now the emergency lights of the vehicles were on. Spotlights shone on a house. We parked and ran back to the scene. Wags was quick on his feet, and managed to get the only video of an officer carrying the baby out of the home.

In the hours after, we learned that there had indeed been a gunshot. The suspect had killed herself as the police approached. All night long there was a dig in the garage of the home where the woman had buried her victim. Now, the story went international. I still find it unbelievable. Sadly, there were a couple of copycat crimes in the months after this happened.

The murdered woman and her husband were members of a very tight-knit, and very protective church in the area. The baby, referred to only as Baby Oscar, was never exposed to any spotlight other than the one shot Wags got. Some months later the father was remarried in a relationship lined up by the church. I only pray that it is best for Baby Oscar, who might not even know of the circumstances surrounding his start in life.

UNDERCOVER

WHEN DOING INVESTIGATIVE WORK, FOLLOWING up tips about consumer problems is usually easy. The process is simple: The tipster relates an experience they had that was negative. After you get their side of the story, then you ask the other party for their side. If that party doesn't respond to a polite request for a comment, maybe you confront them. But when the tip is about something other than a consumer complaint, it gets harder. Many times you must go undercover.

Undercover assignments led to some of the more dangerous experiences I have had. For example, in 1980, while parked in a van at a truck stop outside Youngstown, recording video of women going truck to truck soliciting truckers, we were shot at. It was a warning shot, but still. The shooter made his point and we left. (Luckily, by then we already had enough video to document what was going on. That story was called "The Highway Honeys.") Another example.

Ten years later, in Cleveland's Central neighborhood, photographer Steve Pullen and I were parked and in the back of our van getting footage of drug deals in the King Kennedy public housing complex. We got video of deal after deal. Then we got too bold and moved a little closer. We heard the shot skip off the ground not far from our van. Point taken. We left!

Of course, undercover adventures also lead to some of the funnier experiences I have had, too.

Here are a few of my favorite undercover stories . . .

SAFETY IN NUMBERS

I got a call one day saying that a guy had been evicted from his apartment on Cleveland's near West Side. While he was at work, the landlord had put all his belongings on the front lawn. Neighbors were going through the pile and taking whatever they wanted. I thought it would be an easy story: just watch for a while and confront the thieves. I liked quick stories like this one because they allowed me to appear on the news three or four times a week (the more often people see you on TV, the more news tips you get) while still reserving time for larger-scale investigations. I wasn't scheduled to be on-air that day, so I jumped at the story.

As we approached the address of the apartment, even from a distance we could see what was going on. We parked, got out with the camera, and made our way closer through back yards across the street. We got the video quickly. Then, I noticed, behind a home on the other side of the street, Carl Monday from Channel 8's I-Team. Carl saw me at the same time, and we laughed. Then, we signaled to each other that we had enough video and we all went out to confront the people taking the evicted guy's stuff. Some of those guys had clearly been drinking, though, and became aggressive, approaching us with beer cans in hand. The first thing one guy said was, "You don't look like much." *Here we go*, I thought. Luckily, because there were four of us, we had a stand-off, and we left before things escalated. Carl Monday and I were always competitors, but we were also friends—and on that day we were backups for one another.

LINNDALE

I received a tip that said officers in Linndale, a notorious speed trap on I-71, were sleeping while parked on the highway. I scouted out a location above the highway from which I could look down on it. It was behind a store where I could see the spot where the Linndale cops parked on the berm. I arranged with photographer Chris

Koonz to meet at midnight in a nearby Burger King parking lot. I got into the van, and Chris drove to the spot behind the store, and we began to watch. The police car was there as it usually was, but I couldn't tell if the officers inside were sleeping. I didn't see them stop any cars for speeding, though, so I thought it was a possibility. The police car we were watching drove off after an hour or two, but not chasing anyone. I figured it was a lunch break or something. It was about 2:30 in the morning.

Suddenly, two police cars drove up and blocked us in, one from the front and the other from the back. We were busted! The officer in the front car approached our van and before even seeing me said, "Mr. Orlousky, what are you doing tonight?" What else could I say? "Watching you." He kept it simple and said he hoped we would have a nice night. Then he added, "We saw your car at Burger King and wanted to make sure you were OK." There was no point in us continuing our surveillance. Chris and I left.

I had decided to park my car at the Burger King because it wasn't close to our surveillance spot—in case they were to run my license plate. But it turned out that a car parked there at that time of morning was unusual, so they ran the plate. I have to admit, it was heads-up community policing—but it was also the end of our news story!

MY WIFE GOES UNDERCOVER

I had a tip that a suburban chiropractor was handing out prescriptions to patients who shouldn't be getting them. Surveillance was in order. We had cameraman Chris Koonz checked out by a reputable doctor who also did an X-ray. Chris was fine, no back problems. But we didn't want to send him alone to the chiropractor. We needed a witness and someone to take video. So I recruited my wife, Kim, to go in with him, posing as his wife. She carried a purse with a camera in it.

When Kim and Chris got to the examination room, the doctor did an exam and even an adjustment. Then he said he'd need Chris to take much of his clothing off to continue. Kim is a very proper person, and Chris was a stranger to her, so this wasn't going to happen! They talked their way out of it.

I don't think Kim was comfortable with the close call, but years later we laugh about it. And she got excellent video that made for a great story.

The chiropractor, by the way, was convicted on dozens of insurance fraud, drug, theft, and other charges. He did more than two years in prison.

MICHAEL LEVINE

Michael Levine was charged, along with an accomplice, of murdering Julius Kravitz, the head of Pick-N-Pay, a large supermarket chain in Cleveland in the 1970s. Kravitz's wife was wounded in what was a kidnapping for ransom scheme. The Kravitzes were large donors to many charities and well known in social circles, and the story got a lot of news coverage. Levine was found not guilty by reason of insanity and was sent to a state psychiatric hospital. There was widespread outrage over the not-guilty finding. People asked repeatedly "Can he really get out someday?"

After many years, Levine began petitioning the court, saying that he was sane and should be let out. He would be returned to Cleveland from various mental institutions where he was housed for court hearings on his petitions. Every time he was scheduled to be in court, the night before I would do a stand-up outside the Cleveland Psychiatric Hospital, a foreboding, scary-looking place, and tell viewers that he was back in town asking to be set free. It rekindled the anger over the not-guilty verdict, and to be honest, that is why we did the story. Tapping into that anger generated viewership, which translated to advertising—and that pays the bills.

Levine would be denied each time. A couple of times he wrote me letters afterward. I didn't think to save them, and my only recollection of them is that he was unhappy with my coverage.

In 1993, Levine was judged sane. The verdict against him had been "not guilty by reason of insanity" and now, because he was no longer insane, he would be set free. About a week later, my news director said, "Go find Michael Levine."

Talk about a needle in a haystack! He could be anywhere. But I knew Levine had been held at a state facility in Kettering, Ohio, not far from Dayton. I began checking records from that area, and as luck would have it, he had applied for a driver's license that week. I had his address. Time to get the surveillance van out again.

Cameraman Mark Saksa and I set up camp outside Levine's apartment. I was behind the wheel, ready to follow him; Mark was manning the camera in the back. After an hour or two, Levine came out and we followed him hoping to see what his day was like. At a red light, I lost him. Bummer. We got a bite to eat and went back to Levine's apartment—and found that the window shades were now drawn. Bummer again. Had we returned directly to the apartment, we would have gotten him. We waited for a couple of hours, but there was no sign of him. We checked into a hotel and then went to a Dayton sports bar that we heard was famous for its wings.

Mark and I were sitting at the bar having a beer and some chicken wings when I saw Mark's eyes get as big as saucers. He gave me a look that said, *Stay cool*, then a head nod indicating that there was something important behind me. It was Michael Levine!

Because Levine had written me letters after seeing my news reports about him, I feared he'd recognize me. We made a quick exit. Later, we got video of him bowling, socializing, and doing other ordinary stuff. The point of the story was simple: Here was the triggerman in a murder, out on the town while his victim was dead. Stories about Levine had already resonated every time with viewers, and getting him on camera would be a ratings bonanza.

The next morning, we camped out behind his apartment under an overhang like you see at many apartment complexes. Mark had driven there and had moved to the back of the minivan to shoot whatever happened. He would record audio on a wireless microphone I would be wearing when I jumped out for a confrontation.

I also had a shoulder bag carrying a camera that I would use to get close-up shots.

Levine came out of the building carrying a plastic bag of garbage and went to the dumpster. I moved toward him. I told him who I was, and he said, "I'm not commenting on anything." He got in his car and took off. I returned to the news van, threw the shoulder bag on the passenger's seat, and put the van in gear. What I didn't know was that when Mark drove in, he had parked next to a metal post holding the overhang up. I couldn't see it because we had placed a cloth over the windows, held in place by Velcro. When I turned the wheel sharply to back out and follow Levine, I heard a loud thud. I had hit the post. I straightened the van out, and the chase was on.

As we raced away from the apartment building, I was already complaining about all the paperwork I'd have to do when we got back to Cleveland because of the van damage. The shoulder bag on the passenger's seat had caught the whole thing. We caught up with Levine a couple of miles away in a shopping plaza parking lot. When I approached him again, he said, "This isn't gonna happen." I said all we wanted was an interview and that his tone wasn't making him look good. Why not sit down and talk? He then agreed to sit down later at his apartment. That made me suspicious. Was he playing me? I reasoned that I had already recorded our confrontation, so at least I had something to air if he backed out of the interview. I took a chance and trusted him. In fact, he met us as promised and we got the interview. Levine still was not happy with me because of the chase and the stories he'd seen over the years. But he appeared calm and collected and spent most of the time saying he had paid his dues and lived up to what he was sentenced to serve. Technically, he was right. Eventually the criminal insanity laws changed so this couldn't happen again.

BEGGING FOR TROUBLE

A viewer called to say that a driver who worked for a local charitable organization was keeping some of the donated items that he picked up at people's homes. I got the driver's name, what kind of car he drove, and where he would go to get the truck he used for work. We were there when he arrived as predicted one morning and got into the truck. We followed and watched from a distance, taking notes on each item he collected. At the end of the day, we went back to where he had parked his car and watched as he cherry-picked items he wanted and put them in the back of his station wagon. He was careful to cover the items with a blanket. The stuff he didn't want, he delivered to the charity. We followed him for two days, and the pattern continued.

While he was gone, we were able to see some of the items that had not been completely covered by the blanket. This was important because the tipster also told me that the driver had a booth on weekends at an open-air flea market, where he would sell the donated items that he took.

On a Saturday morning, we went to the flea market at a closed drive-in movie theater in Brooklyn, Ohio. First, we went in without a camera to see if any of the items we had seen the driver take were for sale. They were—lots of them. Now, out came the camera and we confronted him. He was not happy, and as I expected he denied everything, saying that the items belonged to his grandmother and other relatives. Then I told him that we had recorded video of him taking the stuff. It was as if I hit him in the gut. He lit a cigarette, leaned over a fence facing away from me, and looked defeated. I had enough for my story, and it was time to leave before I started looking like the bad guy instead of the real bad guy who had been stealing from the poor.

BIG PERSONALITIES

PRINCE

It was August 1984, and Prince was on the cover of *Rolling Stone*. I had a tip that he was coming to Cleveland to visit his girlfriend, Sheila E., who was appearing at the legendary Agora club in Cleveland. I wanted to cover it for the station, but the news director wasn't too hot on the idea. Pop culture was becoming king, though, so I pushed for the story and he agreed to let me see if I could find this crazily elusive guy, Prince.

My tipster was a limo driver named Richie, whom the station used to bring stars to appear on our various talk shows. A lot of folks ignored Richie, but I always chatted with him about the stars he knew and stuff like that. One day, he pulled me aside and said that he was to pick up Prince at Burke Lakefront Airport. It is a secondary airport close to downtown, used largely for private flights, so the tip made sense. Richie said if he had been working for the television station he wouldn't have told me, but this was a side job.

My plan was to cover two fronts. I had one cameraman go to the Agora in case Prince landed instead at Hopkins International Airport, which had more difficult access to private planes—I would never get Prince there. I went to Burke. I was covered either way, but it turned out that the tip was correct.

At exactly the time Richie told me it would arrive, a private jet landed. A limo-style van approached the plane. A big, burly guy got out of the plane. Chick Huntsberry was Prince's personal bodyguard—nearly 400 pounds, 6'8", and a bruiser. He came over to me and cameraman Tom Livingston. "Sorry guys, no pictures,"

Huntsberry said. I explained that we were here to take pictures and didn't want any problems. He didn't take kindly to that. In a far more aggressive tone, he said "Prince don't want any f***in' pictures." I explained that we had every right to be there, it was public property (in those days you could walk right onto the tarmac), and that we weren't there to hassle him.

Huntsberry wasn't pleased. He grabbed me by the collar of my shirt and my tie and pulled me about an inch from his face and said, "I told you: Prince don't want any f***in' pictures, smart mouth." Next, he threw me to the ground as if I were as light as a softball. Two other muscular guys came out of the plane to block Tom's—and the camera's—view. But to Tom's credit, he got a shot of Prince despite them. It was just the beginning.

Richie had given me another piece of valuable information. A stretch limo would be used as a decoy car; they hoped that anyone who knew Prince was in town would follow that. But Richie was driving the shuttle bus-type vehicle that was actually carrying Prince. With Richie's help, I had planted a wireless microphone in the shuttle bus.

Once I got off the pavement where Huntsberry had tossed me, we ignored the limo and followed the shuttle bus. They drove through the streets of Cleveland, through red lights and the wrong way down one-way streets. I was driving and Tom was shooting video from the passenger seat. He could hear what was going on in the limo, thanks to the wireless mic. "They are really pissed that you found out and that we're following the right vehicle," Tom said. I guess that made us even; I was angry about how roughly I had been treated at the airport. "Let me know when you have enough video," I said. We followed for a few more blocks, and when Tom said he had enough, we headed to the Agora.

At the Agora I made a mistake. I was angry because I had torn my pants and, if memory serves me, had a bloody knee or two. About five minutes later, the shuttle bus showed up. We were positioned perfectly for our coverage because I now had the other cameraman, Jim Gates, at the Agora in addition to Tom. Huntsberry was the first one out of the vehicle. He stared in our direction. Due to my anger, I put on a big smile and gave him a happy wave worthy of Mr. Rogers, kind of like, *How are ya? I'm still here.* It was as if I put a match to a Roman candle!

Huntsberry came at us like a bull. "Come on, come on, come on," he challenged the cameramen as he attacked first one and then the other, swinging wildly and punching. The problem for him was that as he attacked each cameraman, the other one was recording the attack. We had it all on video. It made for a great story.

It also made for a lawsuit. I had the torn pants and bloody knees. Tom got a black eye from where Huntsberry punched the camera and forced it back into his eye. Jim suffered a torn ligament in his camera arm after Huntsberry pushed it to the side and Jim tried to save it. Cameras were very heavy in those days.

For Jim's lawsuit, I was deposed, as was Prince. Jim won a judgment that is under seal, as I understand it. Huntsberry died in 1990.

ALBERT AND OREL

I met lots of famous people over the years. Most were genuinely nice people who were easy to deal with. Some were more difficult.

The owner of a baseball card shop was selling 8x10 autographed pictures of several Cleveland Indians players. I was told that the autographs were fakes. We went to the store and I gave the cameraman money to buy a couple. I told him to get one of Albert Belle, who was the hottest player in the league at the time as well as one of the most volatile, and one of Orel Hershiser, who was one of the nicest guys on the team. My plan was to show the pictures to both players. I figured that if the sulking Belle would say no, I'd have a backup in Hershiser.

I called the Indians and got the OK to go to the locker room. I was escorted in by one of the team's media relations folks. I went for Hershiser first because he was the closest to me. The media relations guy introduced me, and I showed Hershiser the picture. He wasn't interested in talking. He did say it wasn't his signature but wouldn't comment further. I was surprised.

Next it was on to the moody Belle. When I asked the media relations guy to take me over, he shook his head and said, "You're on your own with him." I went over, introduced myself and showed Belle the picture. He talked up a storm! He said it wasn't his signature, wanted to know where I got it, and then started telling me about all the other fake stuff people were selling by using his name. Albert was no dummy. He knew there was money in this merchandise and that other people faking his signature diluted the value of the stuff.

My story was made. Nobody in the media ever had a conversation with Albert Belle, at least not a civil one. I walked back over to the media relations guy, who now had an astonished look on his face. "Wow," he said, "I've never seen that before. He actually shook your hand when you were done."

I went back to the store, confronted the owner, and got the station's money back. His excuse was that he was told by the person he got the pictures from that they were authentic. An old saying comes to mind: I was born at night, but not last night.

MIKE TYSON

Mike Tyson is the only person I've met who had shoulders almost as wide as he is tall. A man you'd have to be crazy to get in the ring with. He was heavyweight champion at the time. He trained with Don King at King's camp in rural Orwell, Ohio, about an hour east of Cleveland. King was a supporter of Cleveland City Council President George Forbes, who was at the time running for mayor against state representative Mike White. King had Tyson come to town for a Forbes rally.

There were various speakers and then Tyson. He spoke for a bit and then tried to lead a cheer saying, "Who are we for? George Forbes!" He didn't know that he was in the heart of a neighborhood close to where Mike White grew up. Instead of repeating "George Forbes," many in the crowd cheered back: "Mike White." Tyson said, "No, George Forbes." The Mike White cheers grew louder. He tried a couple more times, yelling more angrily: "George Forbes!"

It didn't work, and got worse when he blurted out, "Listen you motherf***ers, it's *George Forbes*." They hurried him off the stage. Mike White won the election.

"BOOM BOOM" MANCINI

Ray "Boom Boom" Mancini was just out of high school and had begun a remarkably successful boxing career when I met him. He was a hometown hero in Youngstown and was gaining a larger and larger following.

In the early days, tickets to his fights were laid out on his mother's dining room table and sorted and sold by the family. Humble beginnings. He didn't have a lot of money, even after he began to get televised fights. Our station's news director had made a connection with Ray, so he offered him the help of the television station. We would tape his fights, then Ray and his manager would come to the station to watch and analyze them. It became a regular occurrence. Our videotape player had slow motion, rewind, and other capabilities that you couldn't have at home. The machine was in my office, so I got to know them both well.

We rooted for Ray, who was one of the nicest guys I've ever met—even at that early age and even with all the adulation that surrounded him. He went on to become lightweight champion of the world. It was an example of what hard work, even from a humble beginning with little backing, can accomplish. Youngstown was, and still is, proud of him, and so am I, four decades later.

SISTER CORITA AND THE CROOK

If God ever sent a saint to Cleveland, she is Sister Corita Ambro, a Catholic nun and member of the Sisters of St. Joseph. Since 1970, she has worked seven days a week, along with Father Joe McNulty, at St. Augustine Catholic Church in Cleveland's Tremont neighborhood. Tremont had once been home to steelworkers and other workers who labored long, hard hours. They came home to be greeted by stay-at-home wives who had dinner ready for them, took care of the four or five kids, and ran the household. It was part of Cleveland's postwar success story. In the 1970s, though, factories began to close, as did other companies, including Republic Steel, Richman Brothers tailors, and other Cleveland staples. The neighborhood changed, and by the time Sister arrived, there was a need for a food pantry. Father Joe and Sister stepped up.

Their efforts began slowly, but grew quickly due to Sister's charm and her willingness to be interviewed on TV ahead of the big meal days like Christmas, Easter, and Thanksgiving. She drew hundreds of volunteers. I probably interviewed her thirty times. These days St. Augustine prepares and serves between 17,000 and 20,000 meals on those three big holidays, at St. Augustine's as well as satellite sites in several neighboring counties. Hundreds more meals are served every day at the church.

In the wake of 2008's massive Cuyahoga County corruption scandal, no one had gotten a comment from Frank Russo, our convicted county auditor. After pleading guilty, he was ordered to do community service while he awaited sentencing to federal prison. Rumor had it that he was serving meals a couple of days a week at St. Augustine's. I sensed the chance of a news "get." Marty and I headed down to St. Augustine's at lunch time.

Finding Frank was easy; he was behind a counter stocking a serving tray. He saw me and ducked into the back. I approached him, and he said little. I consider Sister a friend and would never do anything to offend her, so, not wanting to take it much further or create a scene, Marty and I left. As we headed to the car, I had this feeling that I was about to be confronted.

We were almost to the car when I heard the angelic voice behind me. "Paul." A chill went down my spine. I thought, *Oh my God, it's Sister*. It was. From my days in Catholic school, I am still terrified of nuns. I don't mean that in any bad way. In fact, just about everything they ever confronted me with—and that I denied to them—was true. So I already felt guilty.

I heard that voice again. "Paul." I stopped dead in my tracks, turned around, and it was Sister. She came closer and said, "Paul, you're not going to put us on the news, are you?" I immediately reverted to that fourth-grade-boy demeanor I had when Sister Josalita confronted me about some youthful misbehavior. I sheepishly said, "Yes, Sister. We are." She said nothing, but gave me "that look." I was immediately on the defensive. "Well, Sister, we're not going to say where he was," I said. "We're not going to show any of the homeless, and we don't embarrass anyone. It was just about getting a comment from Mr. Russo." The "look" continued from her. After a few seconds that seemed like a few minutes, she said, "I know you'll do the right thing, Paul." Her eyebrows raised as if to say, "Get it?" I did. We showed the interview with no reference to where Russo was.

I had another news "get" moment involving Sister Corita in 2019. Her fundraising had gotten so big that a popular restaurant, TownHall on West 25th Street, started having celebrities come and serve meals to the homeless. It was a kickoff for the holidays at St. Augustine's. People would donate, and media folks, sports celebrities, and others would serve meals and do "meet and greets" with folks. That drove the donations even higher. The restaurant owner, Bobby George, donated heavily as well. We always covered this event, but this time there was a secondary motivation.

Former Browns quarterback Bernie Kosar would be there, as he always was. He and I went back more than forty years to when he was the star quarterback at Boardman High School and I was the news anchor on a Youngstown TV station. The "get" this time, however, was that current Browns defensive end Myles Garrett would be there. Just four days earlier during a game on *Monday Night Football*, Garrett had hit Steelers quarterback Mason Rudolph in the head with a helmet during a fight at the end of the game.

More big names were at TownHall too: Browns quarterback Baker Mayfield, UFC fighting champ Stipe Miocic (a firefighter in a Cleveland suburb), former Indians slugger Travis Hafner, and many others. But Garrett was, no doubt, the "get."

I knew the owners of the restaurant well, so I didn't want to make their guest, Garrett, feel uncomfortable. And of course, in the back of my mind there was Sister Corita. I couldn't take "that look" again. She was at the door greeting everyone who arrived, including me. In fact, I did a quick interview with her when I got there.

When Garrett arrived, Marty and I were the first to get to him amid the crush. He entered quickly and blew past everyone. I had to get something for broadcast, so I said "Myles, nothing about football, just talk to me about this event and your community involvement." He stopped and talked. Owner Bobby George gave me "that look" but didn't object. I got some good sound, and when the other reporters caught up and began to ask about football, they got nothing; Bobby George cut it off.

Sometimes being confrontational isn't the way to get a story. Just one of many lessons learned from the humble and selfless Sister Corita.

JOHN DEMJANJUK

I BEGAN COVERING THE JOHN Demjanjuk case when I got to Youngstown in the late 1970s. Demjanjuk was a retired Ford autoworker who came to the United States after World War II, settled into a working-class neighborhood in Seven Hills, Ohio, and raised a family. In 1976, he got a knock on the door from the United States government. It was the Office of Special Investigations, the Nazi-hunting unit of the federal government. It changed his life and his family's life forever—and it began a story that would grab headlines in Cleveland, and then nationally, and then internationally, for years.

John Demjanjuk was accused of being a notorious Nazi death camp guard called Ivan the Terrible. What an accusation! Ivan had been a brutal guy. One who reportedly beat Jews on their way to the gas chambers at several Nazi extermination camps. He used a rifle to bash them and used his bayonet to cut off ears and noses, and commit unspeakable other atrocities.

I was working in Cleveland by the time the case really heated up. I became intimately familiar with the case and the Demjanjuk family's fight to clear his name. Eventually, I went to Israel for several weeks to cover his trial, conviction, and sentence to death by hanging.

I will present elements of the case from my own perspective. (For those who want more details, numerous books have been written on the subject, and the documentary *The Devil Next Door* offers extensive coverage.) My opinion has shifted back and forth over the years.

I had little contact with Demjanjuk himself over the years. Understandably, he shunned the spotlight, considering the hideous accusation against him. He had a very capable son, John, and a son-in-law, Ed Nishnic, who together fought vigorously on his behalf. They countered every new allegation, faced the media questions every time we asked, and dug up evidence that had been denied to the family and its lawyers, even going into dumpsters outside a former Office of Special Investigations office in New York to find documents that pointed at another suspect.

THE ISRAELI CASE

The Demjanjuk case had three elements. The first government allegation against him was that in 1954 he had lied on his citizenship application about his wartime activities. That allegation triggered a denaturalization case that went on for years. Eventually, Demjanjuk was stripped of his citizenship. Next came Israel's request to extradite him. It took as many years. It was granted and then an order was necessary to deport him. Finally, in 1986, the deportation order was granted as well.

To cover the story, I went to the airport as his family boarded a flight to New York City to visit Demjanjuk a final time. A cameraman and I quickly bought tickets and got on board with them. Demjanjuk was being held in a federal facility in Manhattan, within sight of the Statue of Liberty. The trip would prove fruitless for the family because they weren't allowed any contact with Demjanjuk. They could only watch, crying, as his plane took off from JFK for Israel. Seeing this up close gave me a special insight into the case.

It is easy to paint Demjanjuk as a monster. If he was Ivan the Terrible, that label is true. Yet if he was, he hid it well, including, I believe, from his family. Their anguish, after all the years of legal ups and downs they had endured, was palpable that night. They weren't putting on a show. They were heartbroken by an allegation that they couldn't imagine—a claim that their husband and father, the man who raised them and had cared for them, was capable of the horrible allegations he was charged with.

THE TRIAL IN JERUSALEM

Now came the trial in Israel. It was held in late 1987 and early 1988, in a courtroom that had been constructed in what had been a large theater. News organizations from around the world covered it. I represented NBC News at the trial. In the upper parts of the arena, in the areas outside the actual courtroom, classrooms were set up. School children came to watch the trial and were taught about the Holocaust. The State of Israel admitted that this was totally intended to be a show trial, one that was intended to make an impression on the youth: "Never forget." That said, I don't know how or if that affected the outcome of the trial. There was certainly a fervor in Israel at the time over Demjanjuk.

The courtroom was emotionally charged every day. Survivors pointed at Demjanjuk and identified him. One, Eliahu Rosenberg, identified him. Later, the defense produced a document from 1948 that John Jr. and Nishnic had found. It was signed by Rosenberg, swearing that another man was Ivan the Terrible. Pinchas Epstein, another survivor, provided vivid testimony about Ivan. But there were also serious questions about his possible dementia, given some of his statements. One came when Epstein was asked by the defense how he once got from Israel to Miami. He said, "by train." When questioned further, he said it again.

Ultimately, a three-judge panel found Demjanjuk guilty of murder and crimes against humanity and sentenced him to hang. Demjanjuk appealed. Five years later, his conviction was reversed by the Israeli Supreme Court. He was found guilty of being a collaborator with the Nazis. In simple terms, he was sentenced to time served.

Now, John Demjanjuk was coming home!

BACK IN CLEVELAND

Every reporter in Cleveland prepared an intense search for Demjanjuk. We knew he would be coming home, but how and where? He could land anywhere in the United States. I spent days running down tips all over Northeast Ohio. No luck. For all we knew, maybe he was already home. Radio reporter Carmen Angelo played a hunch one day and went to a small airfield in Medina named, ironically, Freedom Field, and he saw Demjanjuk return on a small plane. He didn't get an interview with Demjanjuk, but Congressman James Traficant, who escorted Demjanjuk home from Israel, did speak. A great exclusive for Carmen.

This turned up the heat on me. I was the Demjanjuk coverage guy for Channel 3. Bosses asked every day, "When will he go back to his home in Seven Hills?" It went on for weeks. I continued looking at places I thought he might be or where tipsters thought he might be. No luck. I put out word to everyone I could think of.

One morning at 11:30, I was working with cameraman "Cowboy" Joe Butano in downtown Cleveland when I got a call from a police source. "Demjanjuk is coming home at exactly noon. This is like a military maneuver; it will be exactly at noon."

I was pumped up but afraid I'd miss it. Depending on traffic it was a good twenty-five or more minutes from where I was to Demjanjuk's home in Seven Hills. I told Joe where we had to go, and that we needed to hurry. Trouper that he was, he ran every light he could and sped down I-77, getting us there at about three minutes before noon. We pulled into a driveway across the street and a couple of doors down from Demjanjuk's house.

As we got out of the car he said, "Hey, let's go over there"—a couple of houses closer. I explained that we didn't want to be seen and that we should just set up and get what we could. This was going to be a huge exclusive. Joe still wanted to move. It was a minute before noon. I almost begged the strong-willed Butano. "Joe, just set up here—this is happening in seconds." I didn't get the words out of my mouth when I saw a police caravan coming down the street. "Joe, here they are!" Joe's camera was still on the ground. He reached down, raised it up . . . and got some very fuzzy video of the arrival. My exclusive was still an exclusive, but—well, the Associated Press story about Demjanjuk's return said, "Video from WKYC Television in Cleveland *purports* to show Demjanjuk returning to his home."

Later that day, it got back to me that the police chief who had been at the Demjanjuk homecoming was angry that I had found out about it, and he was looking for me. I went to his office wondering what was up. He was royally pissed off and his message was simple: "If you go up to Demjanjuk's door again, I'll have you arrested." I never did. However, I believe the chief had gone well beyond his rights to threaten me, because no one in the Demjanjuk family had ever told me not to come to their door.

THE GERMAN CASE

A few years after Demjanjuk returned home to Seven Hills, Ohio, the U.S. Office of Special Investigations files from the earlier case were taken up by Germany, and Demjanjuk was indicted there on tens of thousands of charges. He was being sent to Germany for trial.

Demjanjuk claimed that he was too ill to travel and that he could hardly walk. The U.S. Department of Justice claimed that this was not true. I wondered about it. If you have ever seen a story about Demjanjuk in Israel for the first trial, you've seen the video of him after his 1988 conviction. In the video, he was wearing a blue suit and falling back into the arms of guards as if collapsing. I was standing right there behind the camera when it happened. That is what tweaked my interest in his health claim.

I obtained copies of federal affidavits that are required to get a search warrant on a person. It turned out that the feds had done surveillance on Demjanjuk, and the affidavits were part of the new case file. Some interesting facts were presented to back up the federal claims that he was not too ill to travel. They said that agents had seen Demjanjuk at a certain location at a certain time on a certain date walking with little or no aid. On a date two weeks later, their surveillance showed the same thing at the same location and same time. Based on those statements, playing a hunch, I reasoned that he probably had a doctor or some sort of other appointment every two weeks at that location.

Marty and I went to the location on what would likely be the next appointment date, and my hunch proved true. Here came Demjanjuk, with his daughter next to him. He was walking very slowly but unaided toward the office building. We got video for a few seconds, and then I approached. "Mr. Demjanjuk, can we talk to you?" He looked up, took a couple of more steps unaided, and it seemed to me that when he realized that we were taping him, he started that same groan and collapse I had heard and seen in Israel at the conviction more than twenty years earlier.

Demjanjuk was a big man, bigger than I am, and I am 6'1" and 190 pounds. When he fell back, his daughter grabbed him by the arm as if to hold him up. There is no way she could have done this with one arm. He was too large a man. She said, "Paul, he's seen your stories. He'll never talk to you."

I can't say I am sorry for the confrontation. It was important for Cleveland to see. It changed my opinion to some extent because it was the same thing I had seen previously. Was it an act? I can't be sure, but I was more convinced that he may have been acting than I had been previously.

THE DEMJANJUK FAMILY

I am sorry for the torture Demjanjuk's case put his family through. They are good, honest people who loved someone labeled with a name they couldn't fathom—certainly not from their lives and experiences with him. The day the confrontation story aired, John Jr. wrote me an email scolding me and telling me that I should never contact him or his family again. He remembered our old relationship and having a beer at the hotel in Israel, and he felt I had betrayed it. I hope he is wrong, but I respect how he feels. At times, telling the whole story costs you things you value—like those good people's friendship.

One thing I do know after decades of covering the Demjanjuk case: If he was Ivan the Terrible, only he knew for sure. There are compelling arguments both ways. Lawyer, professor, and researcher Lawrence Douglas may have hit it on the head with his book title and analysis of the Demjanjuk case: *The Right Wrong Man*. It is a title as confounding as the Demjanjuk case.

After that final confrontation with Mr. Demjanjuk, I have had no contact with the family per their request. Demjanjuk was sent to Germany, was convicted, and died there in 2012.

MY BIG MOUTH

I GOT TO WORK ONE day and it was snowing hard outside. Julia on the assignment desk asked if I would run upstairs, get in front of a camera that was showing a static weather shot, and do a downtown update. That was easy enough.

I got there and plugged into the system so that I could hear when they came to me or if they asked me a question. I noticed that, as usual, streets were unplowed and slush-covered. I talked for a minute or so and ended with a line that I thought was funny: "But I hear that Mayor Jackson has a plan for snow removal that is sure to work. It's called spring."

The anchors laughed. Hell, it was a story about the weather, and it wasn't a blizzard—just a winter storm in Cleveland. But a couple of weeks later I was at City Hall for an event and I felt a punch to my arm. It was the mayor's press secretary. I turned and looked at her wondering what was up. "Spring!" she said. "Hey, it was a funny line," I protested. "Yes, it was," she said. "But we didn't like it." We both smiled.

JIM AND TAMMY FAYE BAKKER

Most of my many embarrassing moments over the years were self-inflicted. This one happened at WICZ.

Nick Horsky was my cameraman when I came in at 10:30 each morning. We'd go out, do a story or two, and I'd come back and begin to write and produce the 6 p.m. newscast. One day the mayor was having a big press conference at 11 a.m. sharp. Nick was running audio for the live broadcast of *The PTL Club*, the Christian show. Hosts Jim and Tammy Faye Bakker were live in the studio. The show usually aired on videotape, but during this week it originated from our studio and was also broadcast on several stations in upstate New York. It was a special broadcast designed for them to localize their pitch for donations. I was told that Nick had to stay until 11 a.m. when the broadcast ended. I was furious. I was going to miss the mayor's announcement!

When 11 a.m. came, I headed with Nick toward the studio. We had to go through the studio to reach the steps leading down to the parking lot on the back side of the station. With a stream of profanity coming out of my mouth, I kicked the studio door open, swearing all the way. As I did this Jim, Tammy Faye and their group were standing in a circle holding hands with their heads bowed, praying. Bakker looked up at me, clearly having heard much of my tirade. I kept walking and simply said, "Have a great day."

Like so many of my embarrassing moments, it was my own fault.

MIKE LOVE

I was assigned to cover Ronald Reagan's Inauguration in January 1985. There were local ties. The Brunswick High School band was going to march in the Inaugural parade, as was the Medina County Sheriff's mounted unit.

I flew to Washington with cameraman Rich Geyser, and we were all set to go. One problem: It was only two degrees outside. Because of the temperature, the swearing-in ceremony would be held, but the parade was cancelled. I had to come up with something for the news on the eve of the Inauguration, so we did a story about the weather and all the parade preparations.

One of those preparations was security. I was in front of the White House, standing in the street showing how the sewer caps were wired down so no one could throw a smoke bomb or anything else in there to disrupt the now-canceled parade. Pretty innocent by today's standards, don't you think? No doubt, the world has changed!

In any case, it was frigid. I kept messing up my on-camera "stand-up" due to the cold. Limos were passing by on both sides of us. I tried and tried again. Finally, I was just about through a good take when a guy jumped out of one of the limos and said, "Hey, how you doin' man? Where you from?" He was wearing a full-length fur coat and had long blond hair. He had messed up my one good take. Frustrated, I said, "Hey pal, why don't you take a hike?" (I may be leaving an expletive out, if I'm not mistaken.) He put his hand out and said, "Hi, Mike Love of the Beach Boys." I was embarrassed so I quickly said, "Sorry about that Mike. Can we talk to you a minute?" He agreed. We talked, and when the traffic cleared he headed back toward the limo, waved at our camera, and said, "'MMS rocks! See you at Blossom this summer." WMMS in Cleveland was one of the leading rock radio stations in the country at the time, and the Beach Boys were going to appear at Blossom Music Center that summer.

THE RUG

During the trial of Biswanath Halder, the defendant in the Case Western Reserve University murder, Halder wanted to wear his toupee in court. The defense lawyer, John Luskin, a rough and tumble guy and former police officer, had to make a motion before the judge. As Luskin and prosecutor Rick Bell discussed the motion, I saw them looking into a small box. I wasn't sure what was in the box, but I had an idea. I had Marty shoot the conversation. After the hearing, I confirmed with Luskin that the box had contained Halder's toupee. That night in my news story I used the shot of the two lawyers—both of whom were bald—peering into the box. "Both follicly challenged adversaries discussed their views on the issue before speaking to the judge," I announced. The next day at court, out of nowhere I got a punch in the arm. I turned and saw Luskin, who smiled and said, "You know what that's for."

TELLING A VIEWER OFF

A viewer called one night after my story aired. He had a problem with our treatment of the issue. I tried to explain why we covered it the way we did. He didn't buy a word of it. I tried a different approach to explain. That didn't work either. This went on for a few minutes. He threatened, repeatedly, to never watch us again and to watch the other stations' newscasts.

He was getting a bit rude, and I was getting frustrated. After about the seventh time he threatened to watch another station, I said, "Sir, that is why they put a dial on the damn thing." (In those days, most TVs had dials.) No problem, I thought; I had tried to reason with him.

The next day when I arrived at work, I was greeted with a message from the news director: "Ed would like to see you upstairs." Ed Cervenak was our general manager. I knew what was coming. As I walked in, Ed said, "Paul, did you tell a viewer not to watch us last night?" I tried to sidestep his question. "Well, Ed, it wasn't exactly that way." He wasn't buying it. "Don't ever do that again," he said. I didn't.

WATCH WHO YOU SAY STUFF IN FRONT OF

In 1989, a young middle school girl, Amy Mihaljevic of Bay Village, disappeared on a Friday afternoon after school. A frantic search began. Bay Village is a safe bedroom community where I lived with my family at the time. Amy was a year behind our child in school. The next morning, after a middle-school football game, we were driving past the plaza where she had last been seen. A crew from my station was there. I stopped and got out to ask if they knew anything. They didn't.

The reporter was young and inexperienced in my view, but her cameraman, Steve Pullen, was a veteran pro. I knew he'd know that I was joking when I said, "Only two big crimes in Bay Village history—the Sam Sheppard case and this. They haven't been able to solve either one." (The notorious Dr. Sam Sheppard murder case happened in Bay Village.) Steve smiled. It was a stupid thing to say, but everyone in town was frustrated. I figured that was the end of it.

That afternoon my phone rang. It was Steve. "Orlo, you won't believe what she did," he said—referring to the reporter. "We went to interview the police chief, and she asked him, 'Chief, Paul Orlousky says there have only been two serious crimes in Bay Village and you haven't been able to solve either one of them.'" Uh oh. I couldn't believe a reporter could be that dumb. I had some fences to mend.

Monday morning, I called Bay Village Police Chief Bill Gareau on his private line. He answered, and I told him it was me. "Oh, Paul Orlousky, the crime fighter," he said. "Paul, have you solved this for us yet?" I had a great relationship with the chief. He had let me know when some Cleveland police officers had been trying to find personal information about me after the "Car 224" news stories. Although he took the joke I made in stride (he knew the position that reporter had put me in), he now teased me every time I saw him afterward. The teasing went on for a decade—even after he had been elected clerk of courts. I deserved it.

As Ralph Kramden said on *The Honeymooners* TV show, "I got a BIIIGGG mouth!"

1. In Binghamton, circa 1976—riding in my first parade. Later, I rode on an elephant—wish I had a picture of that! My suit said it all: polyester double knit was king. *(WBNG TV)*

2. Great idea: Have Donny Osmond—"America's Sweetheart"—substitute for the vacationing weather person. Didn't work out well for me, though. Never trust Donny Osmond with a Magic Marker. *(WYTV)*

3. Dorothy Fuldheim was a Cleveland TV legend long before I got to TV 5. I learned the hard way a couple of times that she did whatever she wanted—including walking right through a live shot. *(The Northeast Ohio Broadcast Archives at John Carroll University)*

4. I met Jim Traficant in Youngstown, long before he was a sheriff and well before he became a congressional spectacle. He liked me, and I liked him. However, his crimes were as foul as his mouth. He went to prison, but still talked only to me after release. *(Author's collection)*

5. I was never so scared in my life. My backup left me stranded in a hotel room with two prostitutes and a pimp who was angry that I refused to pay in advance for services. He offered two for $240. What would I do with two? *(Author's collection)*

6. A 40-cent battery in my microphone failed, leaving me stranded. Here I am begging for backup in the non-working microphone in my sleeve. *(Author's collection)*

7. *Where were you guys? I almost got my ass kicked!* By the time backup arrived, the pimp and prostitutes were down the elevator. Our news director declined to pay for another try the next night. *(Author's collection)*

8. This was a good place to get a live shot of the action below. But I wouldn't do this today. Once at a protest people rocked the truck, and when you're about fifteen feet off the ground on a top-heavy truck ... *(Courtesy of WKYC, Inc)*

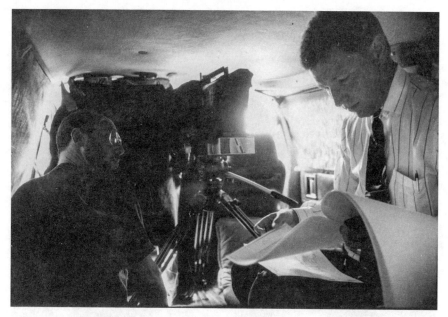

9. My crews were the best. Here we were doing surveillance at a cemetery in 95-degree weather. You can't have the air conditioning on because with the van running you'd be exposed. The only alternative: Crack the windows a bit and sweat for a few hours (or days). *(Courtesy of WKYC, Inc)*

10. The owner of the Crazy Horse was not happy about a story I did about his place. My story was all true, but his sign wasn't. It proved a great way for him to pay me back. Boy, did I get angry phone calls. He still loves remembering this. *(Courtesy of Frank "Al" Spencer)*

11. I was honored to part of this group in 1991, voted by readers to the "Dream Team". Dick Goddard (best weather person), Robin Svoboda (best anchor), Jim Donovan (best sports anchor), and me (best street reporter). Great shot by the late Dennis Innarelli. *(Author's collection)*

12. In Israel for the John Demjanjuk trial. It was an education for me. Military jets flying overhead daily, rifle-toting soldiers on their way to their posts. . . . I've shot my mouth off many times, but never a machine gun. (*Author's collection*)

13. "Prince don't want any pictures," his bodyguard said. I explained that we were there to take pictures. Didn't go over well. I was on the ground, one cameraman had a black eye, another had a torn arm ligament. Chick was an angry guy. (*The Northeast Ohio Broadcast Archives at John Carroll University*)

14. What are your odds of winning a lottery drawing seven times? Pretty long, right? About the same chance as having your named picked out of a stack of Cleveland phone books (Remember those?) twelve feet tall. I proved it and found the cheat. *(Courtesy of WKYC, Inc.)*

15. I would go anywhere to get a story. Here, I'm led underground to explore the sewers below Cleveland. Led me to add willing to go almost anywhere to get a story. What if it had rained? *(Courtesy of WKYC, Inc.)*

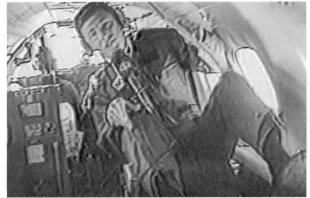

16. They call it NASA's "Vomit Comet" for a reason. I'll leave that to your imagination. Being weightless is like nothing I ever imagined. Barf jokes aside, I'd do it again. *(Courtesy of WKYC, Inc.)*

17. The East Bank of the Flats became a ghost town during the 2008 recession. Old businesses were gone, and financing disappeared for the new developer. How to show that to viewers? Let's go bowling! *(The Northeast Ohio Broadcast Archives at John Carroll University)*

18. I had dreamed of this since I was a kid: floating majestically in the Goodyear blimp over the city. Best of all, on *Monday Night Football*. The ride isn't quite as calming as you might think. *(The Northeast Ohio Broadcast Archives at John Carroll University)*

19. My station softball team played Jimmy Dimora and other Bedford Heights city officials for years. Win or lose, he gave us a trophy. Great guy, great relationship—back then. *(Author's collection)*

20. Years later, I had to chase Jimmy down when he was convicted of serious federal crimes. He was sentenced to 28 years. No trophy. *(Author's collection)*

21. I've been to hundreds of fires and probably a thousand emergency scenes, when you add in crimes. Here I'm with Vic Gideon and Marty Savage. *(Author's collection)*

22. The biggest exclusive of my career: I broke the story of the rescue of Amanda Berry, Gina DeJesus, and Michelle Knight, who had been held captive by Ariel Castro for years. It was only 6 minutes after their rescue—45 minutes ahead of the local competition. The next day the nation caught up. Media row. *(Marty DeChant)*

23. Live shots are unpredictable; you have to watch your back just in case. By my arm and look on my face something must have been going on behind me on Public Square with moments to go live on the air. *(Courtesy of WKYC, Inc)*

MEET SOME NIGHTCLUB EMPLOYEES WHO HAVE SOMETHING TO GET OFF THEIR CHESTS.

According to dancers at local nightclubs, many unlawful activities—like racial discrimination—take place in the clubs where they work.

Starting Sunday, meet these girls and find out the naked truth about what goes on in the strip clubs. Watch Paul Orlousky's undercover investigative report, "The Skin Game," tonight on WKYC-TV Channel 3 News at 11.

Paul Orlousky

24. OK, I did this because it was "sweeps week." Clearly a ratings winner, a sexy story. But it was about a serious issue: racial discrimination at clubs. Everyone lost sight of that fact, though, and I got a lot of heat for it. Great promotional ad, though. *(Courtesy of WKYC, Inc)*

IT'S HARD TO TAKE A BITE OUT OF CRIME WHEN YOU'VE GOT A MOUTHFUL OF DONUTS.

Instead of pounding the pavement, some Cleveland policemen spend their days popping pastries.

Starting Tuesday, Paul Orlousky takes an undercover look at officers who shirk their duties at the taxpayers' expense. Watch our investigative exclusive, "Cream Puff Cops," this week on Channel 3 News at 11.

Paul Orlousky

25. I always regretted doing the story, but I must admit it was the best promotional campaign and title ever: "Cream Puff Cops." *(Courtesy of WKYC, Inc)*

26. My weakest police story led me to meet one of the strongest, yet kindest men on the force, Emil Cielec. *(Cielek family)*

27. Chief Ed Kovacic was "the policeman's policeman"—in my view, the best ever. A friend to the end. That said, he did hold a press conference once just to scold me for twenty minutes in front of every reporter in town. He had the backs of his troops. *(City of Cleveland)*

28. With my long-time cameraman Marty DeChant at the 2016 Republican convention. There is a synergy you need on the streets to keep each another safe. We had it. We also had a good guy/bad guy relationship that worked well for getting stories—and I always got to be the good guy (until we confronted someone). *(Jen Picciano)*

29. With Dan "Wags" Wagner at the Catholic church headquarters downtown. It was the height of the priest sexual abuse scandal. My face says that I wondered if the allegations were true. I was in an odd position. I am a Catholic, and friend to many priests. But that never got in the way of reporting the story. *(Dave Bradford)*

30. This says it all. The town I love and what it has provided to Kim and me. We owe a great deal to Clevelanders for the kindness, love, and support we feel. We weren't born here, but when we arrived 40 years ago it was instantly home. We have always been treated as family here. *(Marty DeChant)*

31. My last day at work—with competitor, collaborator, and friend Carl Monday. We didn't really work together, even at WOIO when we were there together. But even when we were at different stations, we shared a passion: to simply tell the truth. *(Kim Orlousky)*

COURT STORIES

COVERING THE COURTS, PARTICULARLY A long trial, can be boring. And I have covered many of them. But sometimes court proceedings (even those involving serious crimes) can have lighthearted moments. Cameraman Marty DeChant and I have joked for years about many of them. He was no fan of covering court, but he reminded me of some memorable times to write about.

JUDGES PROSECUTORS LOVE

In my experience, Judge Kathleen Ann Sutula was one of the most colorful judges in Cuyahoga County's Court of Common Pleas. A gem; a no-nonsense jurist who often handed out stiff sentences and, when deserved, a scolding to defendants. At times, their lawyers also got the scolding.

I wasn't there, but Marty was in her courtroom one day when she sentenced a man convicted of a crime. He muttered the dreaded F-word to Judge Sutula as he was being taken to the holding cell to wait to be taken to prison. She thought she had heard it, but wasn't sure. She called the deputies who had been escorting the guy back into her courtroom and asked them to repeat what he had said. They thus, reluctantly, had to repeat the F-word. The defendant was brought back, and a re-sentencing date was set for a week later. The defendant was reminded by the judge that she had additional time she could give him, but wanted to think it over. (She later told me recently that such a warning usually did the trick, and the defendant after returning to court was always apologetic. In this particular case, she didn't add on any time.)

Another day, Marty and I were waiting for a proceeding in the courtroom of Judge Daniel Gaul—another judge not afraid to give defendants stern advice at sentencings. He, like Judge Sutula, was trying to make a difference in people's lives by getting them on the right path.

While we waited, Gaul heard the case of a young suburban kid who had been busted for possession of pot. The judge spent a good amount of time explaining to the kid that he was going to set him up in a diversion program. He detailed all that the young man would have to do to have the conviction disappear from his record.

When the proceeding began, he asked the defendant when the last time he used drugs was. "A few weeks ago," the kid said. After a long explanation of the diversion program, Gaul said, "OK, we'll take you downstairs, have you drug tested, and get you started." While he said this, the young man whispered something to his lawyer. Gaul saw it and leapt to his feet. He knew what was up. "Are you going to pee dirty?" he shouted. "I just spent a half-hour trying to help you out, and you're gonna pee dirty, aren't you?" He told the kid the deal was off and ordered him to the holding cell. The kid began to cry loudly. He knew he wouldn't be able to pass the urine test.

Gaul called the next case. It was a streetwise probation violator who had witnessed what happened in the previous case. The proceeding began. One of the first questions from Judge Gaul was, "When was the last time you used?" It was hardly out of the judge's mouth when the guy said, "Last night, your honor." We couldn't help laughing. He had learned fast. His case went far better than the suburban kid's did.

JUDGES DEFENSE LAWYERS LOVE

The Cuyahoga County Courthouse is home to thirty-four judges. Lawyers often joke that while there are thirty-four judges, there are sixty-eight personalities. I'm not sure I agree, but there are certainly varying styles in that building. There are also wide swings in the length of sentences those convicted get, depending on what judge they are assigned. In the morning arraignment room where defendants make their first appearances and are assigned a judge, lawyers are often heard commiserating on this topic. Several times I've heard them say, after drawing Judge Sutula, Judge Gaul, or another judge considered a tough sentencer, "Sorry, tough draw." I once saw a lawyer high-five another after drawing a judge known for his light sentencing practices.

One judge in particular was considered by many to be a light sentencer—a great draw for defendants and a nightmare for prosecutors. One day we were in his courtroom for the sentencing of a man on a rape charge. The guy had sneaked into a young woman's apartment as she was moving in. She had propped the building door open with one of her moving boxes. He hid in a closet until she brought her last box in. He came out of her closet, held a knife to her neck, and raped her.

The judge handed him a long sentence, one of the harshest sentences I'd ever seen him give. Marty and I thought it odd and somewhat out of character. That afternoon, Marty came to my desk with a smile on his face. He had done some research and figured out that the rape had occurred not far from the judge's home. It was the holiday season, and Marty figured that the judge probably didn't want to be seen by his neighbors at a holiday gathering as being lenient in a crime so close to their homes. Not sure if that is true, but it would explain a lot.

A case comes to mind with a different judge who was also seen by prosecutors as giving light sentences. A lawyer from an affluent suburb had been convicted on a pornography charge after kiddie porn was found on his home computer. He lived in a house that backed up to an elementary school playground. He was sentenced to probation and argued that the house near the school was his office, so he could be there—despite restrictions on sex offenders. The judge agreed. Prosecutors weren't happy with the sentence or the living arrangement. A few weeks later, someone called me saying that I should check the docket for the case. I did, and there was a new entry from the judge that said that based on a psychologist's evaluation, the lawyer could look at pornography as he needed it to help him with "sexual release," which was part of his rehabilitation. It said he couldn't access child pornography; only adult pornography. I did a news story exposing that, and that ended my relationship with that judge.

SUBURBAN JUDGES

It is a whole different story when you go out into the suburbs or smaller towns where judges aren't used to having cameras in the courtroom. You get a couple of different reactions. Some are hesitant and make you fill out paperwork and limit where you can be in the courtroom. The media—including me—feels those restrictions are petty. But I'm not the judge.

On the flip side of this, other suburban or rural judges see cameras in the courtroom as an opportunity. They talk and talk and talk, thereby increasing their time on camera. Judge Walter Savage in Parma Municipal Court was the first to figure out the value of being on camera. His courtroom jury box, where cameras were positioned, was on the side of his bench. He had his name plate moved from the front of the bench facing the courtroom to the side of the bench facing the cameras. It was of no use to anyone in the courtroom because they couldn't see it—but it told everyone watching at home exactly who he was.

STANDING UP FOR THE MEDIA—WITH HELP

At times, particularly in juvenile court, I've had to stand up before a judge who was deciding on a lawyer's motion to bar camera coverage. On behalf of the media, I'd cite case law that says cameras can't be barred without a hearing. I didn't know the case law, but I quickly learned, thanks to another reporter. One day we were about to get kicked out of court when *Plain Dealer* reporter Rachel Dissell whispered to me that I should object. I stood up and objected and then cited the case she gave me: "Plain Dealer Publishing vs. Floyd 2006, Your Honor." It worked, and we stayed.

Rachel, a tough, aggressive, and most importantly accurate reporter, had broken huge stories over the years. I was surprised she hadn't stood up and objected herself. She isn't afraid of anything. After the hearing I asked her why she didn't do it. Turns out, she didn't want to be on camera. But she had come to court prepared with what she needed to get the story for her readers. A pro's pro, through and through!

A PUBLIC DEFENDER ON THE ATTACK

Then there is the case of the Chardon public defender who went over the top in defending her client. The client, a woman who had been pulled over for drunk driving, had been caught on a police dashcam during the arrest and had been wearing little clothing. The TV station had aired the video. The client was due in court a day or two later. Marty and I waited but saw no sign of her in the courtroom. The public defender kept coming into the courtroom, looking at us, and leaving. I figured that she had her client tucked away in a conference room or something.

After about the fourth time the lawyer ducked in to look at us, I watched her as she went outside. I reasoned that her client was probably outside in a car. The next time she came back inside, Marty and I went into the parking lot. It was full of cars, and we had no idea which one the client was in until two women in one car suddenly put the sun visors down and began to cover their faces. It was a dead giveaway! We went over to the car and tried to ask questions. No answer. Then the public defender came charging out of the courthouse.

"You guys are the biggest a**holes in the world," was how she began. She believed we had given the video of her client's arrest to one of the tabloid national shows, which had used it on the air. We hadn't; it was a public record available to anyone by simply making a records request.

Marty rolled on the entire confrontation, and the lawyer clearly didn't like it. She took her stack of paperwork and whacked the camera lens with it. Her papers went flying all over the sidewalk. We could have gotten angry, but why? No one was hurt. I knelt and helped her pick up her papers. That made her even madder! A syndicated TV show that reported on odd happenings saw our video of the incident. They picked it up and ran it. They were not the only ones. To my embarrassment, others did, too, although they used a different part of the video.

I decided to get cute that day with my stand-up portion of the story. I was sitting behind the wheel in our parked news car. I had Marty get in the back seat and shoot me in the rear-view mirror, showing only my face. As I began to speak, he pulled out from my face to a wider shot. I wanted to explain what a surprise the arresting officer must have had when the suspect got out of her car wearing little clothing. I had taken my jacket, tie, and shirt off, and now as I spoke and stepped out of the car, the fact that I was topless was revealed as Marty pulled to a wider shot.

The next day I learned the story got noticed, but not necessarily in a way that I wanted. I walked into the newsroom and producer Tamu Thomas, said, "Saw you on *Good Morning America* today." I paused and said, "Let me guess—the shirtless standup?" Yes. I think I blushed. I went out to do my story for the day, and when I returned, someone else told me that it had been on NBC's *Today* show as well. A TV website called FTV carried a headline the next day that read, "Was This the Worst Stand up in Television History or the Best?" You can decide; it is probably still out there somewhere in cyberspace.

As for the public defender, at the suggestion of a former member of the disciplinary council, we made a complaint to the Ohio Supreme Court Disciplinary Counsel. She had to respond, which I am sure was embarrassing to her, but no discipline was taken against her for her attack.

CHARACTERS OF THE COURTHOUSE

I believe I had great relationships with most of the judges and lawyers I dealt with during my career. Many of the judges came from the ranks of the county prosecutor's office, some from private practice. In Cuyahoga County, having a politically popular name helps judges get elected. There have been plenty of Gallaghers, Callahans, Russos, Celebrezzes, and others with familiar and thus very electable family names. TV commentator Dick Feagler once delivered an on-air editorial about this name game saying, "We even elected a Calabrese just because it sounds like Celebrezze."

I can't remember which judge it was, but the first time I saw him after his election I asked how being on the bench was different from being a lawyer. He answered immediately. "I never knew my jokes were so funny," he said. "Since I put the robe on, everyone always laughs at all of them."

Riding up the packed elevators in the Justice Center, you learn to read people. In short, you learn who not to touch, or if possible, not even get close to. Sometimes the elevators smelled of fresh alcohol or last night's pot. The twelfth floor is where the arraignment room is. Those getting off there typically were at the courthouse to answer a criminal charge, be booked, and have a mug shot taken. I developed a game in my head: "Who is Getting off on Twelve?" I got rather good at it. I shared it with Marty, and we played the game together at times, laughing when we got them all right. Not a particularly nice thing to do, but no one got hurt and it gave us a smile when we knew we were heading to a courtroom on another floor for a trial at which some expert would drone on for hours on end.

GOING ON TRIAL IS HUMBLING

One day we went to the arraignment room to cover the case of a doctor who had been arrested and charged with hundreds upon hundreds of violations of the state's drug laws. In effect, the government was saying he was running a "pill mill." The State of Ohio had sent undercover agents into his office to complain of various (fake) ailments. Back pain was a big one. One of those visits lasted less than thirty seconds before the undercover agent was handed a prescription from the doctor for a narcotic pain reliever.

It was clear the state had a lot of evidence. When they raided the doctor's home, they found a currency counter like ones you'd see in a bank. They also found a walk-in safe containing shrink-wrapped bales of money—a half-million dollars in cash, we were told. The home was no bungalow!

When the doctor got to court and saw us taking video, he demanded that we stop taping him. He accosted a court deputy, telling him to stop us. "I'm a doctor," he scolded the deputy. Didn't work. We taped him and the arraignment with no further problems.

Weeks later, I sat in for a couple of hours during his trial. He was still carrying an aloof attitude and defending his position. A few weeks, maybe even a month later, on a Friday, I was at a court case across the hall. During a recess, I poked my head into the doctor's trial. One of his nurses was testifying that he told her to change records and labels on bottles. The prosecutor would ask, "And who told you to do this?" She said repeatedly, "The doctor did." His head was hanging. You could sense he knew he was defeated.

I got a call the next day. The doctor had jumped off a bridge and had died. Several months later, Marty and I were talking to the lawyer who had represented him. He said that he had tried to convince the doctor to agree to a plea deal. He would be given two years in prison and had to forfeit the cash investigators had seized from his home. The doctor had adamantly refused and did not take the deal. It seems the very arrogance we captured on that first day had gotten the better of him.

DOES BAD EVER LEAD TO GOOD?

Typically, bad things bring people to court. But not everything that happens in court is a bad thing. There are occasional success stories, especially with people addicted to drugs. Drug court is one of the specialty dockets. Judges in that court have special training and access to experts to help them choose the course a defendant should take to get better, rather than just locking them up. The news media don't generally cover these stories. I did once. It was a graduation. Former druggies who had turned their lives around were in court for encouragement and a progress report. In this case, it was Judge David Matia's drug court docket.

There were testimonials from the recovering addicts, their sponsors, families, and more. Before-and-after photos were shown. It was inspiring to see. I don't know how many continued their recovery, but such graduations were not held early in their rehab; these addicts were well into recovery. I hope all are still clean and sober. This procedure makes for a far more productive citizen than sending an addict to prison.

A JUDGE WHO WAS A POLICE DECOY

One judge who "got it" was Ellen Connally. She was a Cleveland Municipal Court judge, and from what I saw over the years, she tried to get a real understanding of the circumstances that brought people into her courtroom before she sentenced them. She would ask a lot of questions.

She also went to great lengths to get answers. Her court was being flooded by a large number of prostitution cases. Two kinds of people came before her in these cases: prostitutes and "johns." She was curious and wanted a clear perspective, and she took a unique step to understand the situation. I can't imagine any other judge doing what she did. She went out with the vice unit and watched what went on—and even served as the decoy on a stakeout aimed at arresting johns who were looking for prostitutes. She has a wonderful sense of humor and joked to me once that they stopped using her because no one stopped to proposition her anymore. That wasn't true; that was her keen self-deprecating sense of humor.

Years later, she was retiring, and I went over to interview her. We told stories from knowing each another for twenty-five or more years, but one question I asked made her pause. What was the oddest case she had ever handled? She waited a moment, and said she didn't know, but then said, "I did have a defendant that I sent to prison once as a man, and years later I sent the same person back to prison as a woman." Although I thought I saw a lot as a TV news reporter, these judges really get an eyeful!

TOO HARD ON HIMSELF

Jim Burge was a defense lawyer in Lorain County. He later became a judge. He was always very friendly to me, and he was particularly fond of one of the station's cameramen, Jim "JJ" Jackson. If JJ would walk into Burge's courtroom late, Burge would tell the lawyers to stop, and tell JJ, "Set up over there, JJ. How are you today?" They would chat, and the attorneys would fume. One day I was in Burge's office and noticed a picture of a convicted killer named James Filiaggi hanging on his wall. Filiaggi had been executed for murdering his ex-wife, Lisa. I remembered that Burge had defended Filiaggi at trial before he was elected judge. I asked him about the picture, and he said, "I keep it there to remind me of something. I never want to forget what can happen when lawyers fail to do everything they can for a client." I thought he was being too hard on himself, but the story stuck with me. Years later I called Burge to make sure I had the quote right. He corrected my memory on a word or two. I told him I thought he was being too hard on himself. His response was classic: "If I was easy on myself, I'm not worth a damn."

OOPS!

Smartphones made life easier for reporters in the courthouse. In the hallways outside courtrooms, people who are scheduled for a hearing or for sentencing sit and wait. This is your only chance to get them on camera and ask them about their case. I am embarrassed to tell you that before smartphones, Marty and I confronted the wrong person on several occasions. Your first thought upon doing this is that the person is lying to you. Eventually, though, you realize you've made a bad mistake. You have to back off and say, "Sorry about that!" With smartphones, you can look up their mug shots on the Internet and avoid the embarrassment caused by guessing.

DEFENSE VS PROSECUTOR—LITERALLY

Some criminal lawyers I've met have become hardened by their jobs over the years. Not all of them. One particularly good guy, and good lawyer, is Kevin Spellacy. He was in court one day when there was a dispute between the two sides. Jim Gutierrez was the prosecutor. Gutierrez is a guy whom a lot of defense lawyers don't like. He is a good prosecutor, but many lawyers felt he could be overly direct in his approach.

I couldn't hear what was being talked about during a sidebar over the dispute. I could see that Gutierrez was talking when suddenly defense lawyer Mark Stanton lurched at him saying something like, "Why you—" Other lawyers stopped him, and it was over.

A few months later, Spellacy approached me in the courthouse. "Hey, you were there when Stanton went after Gutierrez, weren't you?" he asked. I said I was. He asked if we still had the video. I knew we did. He asked me for a copy of it because the defense lawyers' group was honoring Stanton with an award and roast the next Friday night. I got the copy for him, and the video was played at the event. It got big laughs, I was told—partly because a lot of defense attorneys have wanted to do the same thing to the aggressive prosecutor Gutierrez.

I didn't see Stanton that often, but in this instance within a couple of days I did. Marty and I were waiting for an elevator at the courthouse. One stopped but was completely full. Right in front of the car was Stanton. He glowered at me and said, not very happily, "Thanks for giving them that tape." I just stood there and let the door close. We got the next elevator.

YA GOTTA DO WHAT YA GOTTA DO

I had an interesting confrontation with a lawyer who was convicted and did time in relation to the 2008 Cuyahoga County corruption scheme. He had been charged with serious crimes. After a hearing one day I followed him through a hallway out of the Federal Courthouse. The hallway led to a parking garage and was off limits to cameras. The parking garage wasn't off limits. I put my partner in confrontation, Marty, on the lowest level, level one. It was Marty's idea. I wasn't sure what level the lawyer had parked on. If the lawyer got off on level two, I was screwed. He gestured that I should get on the elevator first. I did; but what to do? I hit level two, then he hit level one. I knew we had him!

I had questioned him without a camera in the hallway, and he said he had nothing to say. As the elevator lowered to level two and the door opened, he looked to me to get off. I said, "Damn, I made a mistake!" explaining my not getting off. As we continued toward level one, he looked at me and said, "I want to thank you for not getting in my face with a camera." Just then the elevator doors opened, and there was Marty with the lights blaring and the camera rolling. The lawyer looked at me like "you piece of crap." We gave him a chance to speak and he said nothing, but it was only fair to ask. I'm not gonna lie, it was also compelling television!

JUDGE MIKE

One of the most levelheaded guys I ever met was Judge Michael Cicconetti, a municipal court judge in Painesville. Over the years, he gained quite a reputation for creative sentences. They were intended to send a message. He'd sentence nonviolent defendants to work in a community garden during the summer. In the fall, the produce went to food pantries. In recent years, he'd require people convicted of DUI to install Uber and Lyft apps on their phones and attach a credit card in advance. There were many such examples, but the first one I covered was the most memorable.

During his arrest a man had called the police "pigs." Judge Cicconetti found out and wanted to make the point to the guy that this was disrespectful. I think he wanted to make him feel as disrespected as he had made the officers feel. Cicconetti sentenced the man to stand in a pig sty for two hours at lunch time on Painesville's public square. The man had to hold a sign pointing at a real live pig that read, "This is a pig, not a policeman." I always wondered how his bailiff, Nick Cindric, ever came up with a sty, a pig, and a load of straw, but he did.

While standing there watching the spectacle, I saw Leon Bibb from Channel 3 and Gary Stromberg from Channel 8. I laughed. "We've got almost a hundred years among the three of us covering news, and here we are covering a guy in a pig sty with a sign and a pig." Just then another reporter who had been in town for a long time came over and joined us. Now we were up to about 120 years!

"THE PUPPET'S COURT"

It was during the 2008 Cuyahoga County Corruption scandal. Dan Salamone called me into his office at WOIO one day and asked how we should cover the trial. Cameras were not allowed in federal courtrooms. I suggested the obvious—we should get an artist to do sketches. "I'm thinking of doing it with puppets," Dan said. "Give that some thought." *Puppets?* I was dumbfounded. And I did *not* give it some thought, not a moment of thought, because I thought it was crazy.

About two weeks later, around one in the afternoon, Dan called me. "I've got the puppeteers coming in at three. Can you write me up a script?" I was screwed. I hadn't prepared—not for puppets. I quickly reviewed tapes of some of the press conferences and statements that had been made in the pretrial court filings. It didn't flow together at all. How to do it? OK, I decided, how about a reporter puppet to throw from one clip to another?

I found some salacious quotes, had the reporter puppet say things like, "And then in wiretaps Commissioner Dimora said this . . ." followed by a puppet that looked like Dimora repeating the line. That day, they did a rough take of what it would look like on camera. It was not great. My involvement with it was over at that point!

By the time the trial began, Dan had puppets made that looked like the main players in the trial. The puppeteers were more polished. Misty Stiver, a producer, sat in the courtroom and took down quotes. She and reporter Dan DeRoos back at the station crafted the nightly episodes that became "The Puppet's Court." I would do the hard news story at the start of the news; later, the puppets would perform the reenactment of the day.

We feared that we'd be blasted in other media. But an Associated Press reporter, Tom Sheeran, turned the tide the next day. He wrote an article saying that we were making a journalistic point. Why weren't cameras allowed into a proceeding that was this important to Cuyahoga County? The national media picked his angle up. I have always felt that if Tom had gone the other way and mocked us, it could have made us a joke.

Now, I'd go to court in the morning and would hear a prosecutor or attorney say to another, "Hey, I saw you got your own puppet last night." It was a ratings bonanza. Years later, a retired lawyer who led the prosecution team told me that they knew it was time to stop their preparations for the next day when the clock hit 11 p.m. They'd turn the TV on, watch the puppets, and go home.

I did have a question for Dan after the first episode. The reporter puppet was a squirrel. "Dan, people think that's me," I said. "Why a squirrel?" He said, "Well at least it wasn't a weasel."

TWO COLORFUL POLITICIANS

JIM TRAFICANT

There is no singular way to describe Jim Traficant, the abrasive congressman from Ohio. Defiant comes to mind. Compliant never does. I met him when he was on the way up. It was 1979 in Youngstown, and Traficant was the head of a local drug intervention program. Even then, he knew how to get headlines. One time, one of our reporters did a story on his program. Two weeks later, Traficant came to the TV station proudly holding a plaque, a proclamation, as if the reporter had won some sort of award. Actually, he had gone to a trophy shop and had it made himself. Didn't matter: He got another mention on the news of both his name and his organization.

His notoriety grew.

Running for Sheriff

In 1981 he decided to run for sheriff of Mahoning County, which included Youngstown. The Democratic party was king in Mahoning County. Whoever party boss Don Hanni decided would be the nominee in the spring primary election would be the nominee. In the fall, they would always win. Republicans were doomed in the blue-collar Democratic stronghold of what is now the epicenter of the Rust Belt. There was one problem for Hanni: Jim Traficant.

Traficant decided he would run against Hanni's nominee in the primary. He was warned not to do so, but he didn't care about that. He ran and won. Remember, this was the Democratic primary; no one ever challenged the status quo. He bucked the boss, Hanni—unbelievable at the time.

Election night was my first real up-close view of Jim Traficant's style of confrontation. We arranged for Traficant and Hanni to appear on set that night at 11 to report the election results. I was the anchorman. Don Hanni showed up. Then, just before air, Traficant showed up—and he was carrying a big stick. Trouble was about to begin!

The movie *Walking Tall* had been popular, featuring the character Sheriff Buford Pusser, known for his personal war on drugs, prostitution, and the mob. A guy who bucked the system. And who carried a big stick. (It was a take on the Theodore Roosevelt quote, "Speak softly and carry a big stick": "Walk tall and carry a big stick.")

Once we got on the air, without a lot of provocation, Jim started challenging Hanni. Hanni said something, and in reply Traficant brandished his big stick and challenged the party boss: "Hanni, there is a new sheriff in town." He wasn't kidding.

I was completely unprepared to be the live on-air lion tamer in this three-ring circus featuring Hanni the powerful, Traficant the challenger, and me the befuddled.

Traficant was elected sheriff without Hanni's blessing.

The Feds Said He Took Bribes

I encountered Traficant again a few years later. He was now the sheriff—and he now faced a federal charge filed against him saying he had accepted $55,000 in bribe money from Youngstown mobsters. Serious stuff. And he defended himself in court! Just him against the entire United States Justice Department. Everyone thought he was crazy.

Traficant's defense was that he accepted the money from Youngstown's Carabbia brothers, members of a powerful and reputed local crime family who were later sentenced to prison, to keep it out of the hands of the mob. That made no sense. He also claimed that he later returned it. Salacious audio recordings of his meetings with the Carabbias made it clear that Traficant knew what was going on. The tapes were strong evidence against him at trial. There was never any evidence that he returned any of the money.

He was vulgar and defiant during the trial. I was there, and I believe that his strategy was to unnerve the federal prosecutor on the case, a man named Steve Jigger. Repeatedly during the trial, he would refer to him as Mister Jiggers. It drove the guy crazy. He would object every time Traficant said it. I believe it distracted him.

From the very beginning of the case, he was defiant.

It started at a news conference in Youngstown after the initial indictment was filed against him. He looked directly into the news cameras and said, "To all the powerful and influential people in this valley that want me out, I have one thing to say." He paused several seconds making eye contact with each camera. "Go and f*** yourselves." It was carried on TV newscasts live at noon that day.

Later, during the trial after an awfully bad day in court for him, I followed him down the street to try to get a comment. "Look at you, Orlousky, dressed up in that Cleveland anchorman suit," he said. "Come on Sheriff, give me a quote I can use," I said. "I'll give you a quote on how it went today," he replied. "I feel like I had Pac-Man chomping at my hemorrhoids." I didn't use it.

Traficant eventually won an acquittal.

On the day he was acquitted he came out onto the steps of the Federal Courthouse on Superior Avenue in Cleveland and stopped in front of the many cameras there. He looked left and right, directly at each camera, just as he had three years earlier in the Youngstown incident. He didn't disappoint. He rambled a bit, then said, "To all the people here is Cleveland . . ." *Oh boy*, I thought, *here it comes.* ". . . I have just one thing to say." Now I was sure something was coming. He paused and smiled. "Sayonara." Cameraman Dave Arnold and I followed him down the street to try to get more, but all he did was point a finger at us as if it was a gun. He pretended to fire and said nothing. It was later used as the closing shot of an ABC News report on Traficant.

Congressman and Convict

In 1984, Jim Traficant beat the odds once again. He won election to the United States House of Representatives. He changed jobs, but not his style. He quickly became known for his one-minute speeches that pointed out the crazy workings of this or that federal department. Always punctuated them with his catch phrase (lifted from *Star Trek*), "Beam me up."

Eventually the odds beat Jim Traficant. In 2001 he was indicted again, this time for a kickback scheme. Contractors said he demanded kickbacks. So did his employees, who also claimed he had them work for free on his home and boat. He was convicted in 2002.

After his conviction he was kicked out of Congress. A day later we heard that he was at one of his district offices in Canfield, Ohio. Marty and I headed there and camped outside the office building with a dozen other reporters and their camera crews, hoping he'd come out and say something.

As luck would have it, I encountered a former sheriff of a rural Ohio county who I knew was a close friend of Traficant. He was heading inside to see Traficant, but first I spoke with him in the parking lot. Just a pleasant conversation about the past.

About an hour later, out came Traficant. He looked out at the gathered crowd of reporters and said, "I've decided to give an exclusive interview to Paul Orlousky from Cleveland TV. If he wants to share it with ya's he can. If he wants to screw you, that is fine with me too. Now I want ya's to leave, all of ya's. Get out." He turned and went back inside.

Marty and I went in and did the interview. Traficant was his usual confrontational self with us, which surprised me, given what he had just said outside. He just couldn't help being defiant. When the interview ended, though, he smiled and in a far different tone asked how Marty and I were doing. I reminisced a bit about my time in Youngstown. At the end of our conversation he said, "Hey you guys want a flag? I won't be needing 'em." He had boxes of them in his closet. We said sure, and he gave one to me and one to Marty. We both flew them until they wore out.

This was another time when just being a regular guy paid dividends. It should be a lesson to young reporters: Don't make all your source connections via social media. Talk to people. That "small time" former sheriff got me a huge exclusive used on the network news.

Jim went to prison and got out 2009. I never talked to him again. He was fatally injured in 2014 while using a tractor at his daughter's farm. It toppled over on him, and he died four days later. He absolutely was one of the most memorable people I have met in more than fifty years of doing this job.

DENNIS KUCINICH

Dennis Kucinich and I have known one another since 1981. At that time, he was a defeated former mayor of Cleveland known as the "Boy Mayor." He had been only thirty-one years old when first elected. I wasn't in Cleveland when he was defeated or for any of the controversial topics surrounding his time as mayor, but I got to know him well after that.

He ran for a lot of public offices. In 1982, an incumbent Cleveland city councilman died. He represented the ward where Dennis had grown up—Cleveland's Broadway Fleet neighborhood, a Polish ethnic stronghold. How Polish? The future Pope, John Paul II, had visited St. Stanislaus Church in that ward when he was a cardinal in Poland. Dennis had attended grade school at St. Stan's. He didn't live in the ward when he ran for city council, though. But nothing in the rules said he had to. He ran, and he won. In 1985 Dennis left politics for a time to work in the private sector. During that time, he had a couple of unsuccessful runs for governor and the United States Congress. In 1994, Dennis won a seat in the Ohio Senate. Then, in 1996 he was elected to the United States Congress. In 2004 he ran unsuccessfully for President, and he tried it again in 2008, also without success. Yes, Dennis ran a lot.

I have no desire to discuss politics here, and I have no agenda. Dennis was always good for a news story.

During Dennis's 1982 campaign for Cleveland City Council, I covered him on election night and remember it well. The reception was held at a now-closed ethnic spot, The Polish Falcons Club. Polka music was playing in the background while we shot Dennis's triumphant arrival and his speech declaring victory. In his speech he acknowledged by name many of the older Polish women who supported him, and he kissed each of them live on TV. We even had a shot of Dennis hugging his father at his arrival. His dad died only a couple of weeks later.

Watching a tape of that night years later refreshed my memory on what a populist Dennis was. How people responded to him. He also knew exactly how to play to the media!

That night in 1982, during a live talkback segment, anchorman Ted Henry was quizzing Dennis, asking if this council seat was just a platform from which to run for mayor again. Dennis deflected the question a couple of times. Ted was no rookie. He persisted. Eventually, Dennis turned to his adoring crowd and said, "Hey listen to this, everybody. Ted Henry is trying to draft me to run for mayor." They cheered wildly. Ted said, "No I'm not," but the crowd couldn't hear Ted—they only heard Dennis!

When Dennis decided to run for president in 2004, his first stop was Iowa and the caucuses. I flew there with a cameraman. We arrived late, and a Kucinich rally had already begun. Not surprisingly, it was held at an ethnic club. Dennis knows his political base. When we walked in, Dennis was already on stage. He saw us, stopped, and said, "Hey everybody, welcome my friend from Cleveland, Paul Orlousky." The cameraman was new to Cleveland and looked shocked. Later he asked me how Dennis knew my name. "Dennis knows everyone's name," I told him. Dennis was always aware of who was covering him and where they were from.

He dropped out of the presidential race and returned to Congress. He did the same thing in 2008. When Ohio lost two congressional seats in 2013, Dennis's district was put into an area that stretched far west, largely outside of his power base. Much of his newly mapped out district was in Toledo, an area where the Republican-controlled Ohio legislature knew he couldn't win when they drew up the redistricting maps. Dennis lost.

After that he spent time at Fox as a liberal voice on the conservative-leaning network. In 2018, he decided to run for governor of Ohio. The day he made his announcement, cameraman Kevin Rans and I were confused as to which building it would be in. In the parking lot, from a passing car I heard, "Hey, Paul, it's the building over here." It was Dennis. Kevin looked at me in surprise, just as had happened years before in Iowa. "How did he know your name?" he asked. "Dennis knows everyone's name," I said. Again.

With Dennis, it's never over until he says it's over. That leaves me with a suspicion. I don't think it is over for Dennis. Where it will go? I have no idea. A return to the mayor's office? No clue. A return to the private sector? No clue. A return to some other public office? No clue. But it ain't over for Dennis Kucinich. That I do know!

NATIONAL CANDIDATES

IT IS A THRILL TO meet a candidate for national office. They are larger-than-life figures that you've either read about, seen on the national stage, or in one way or another liked or disliked. The job of a reporter is to cover them and not let your personal views get in the way of fair coverage. With that in mind I should tell you, I have never been a member of either political party, and I also have never voted a straight ticket for either party. That is the base from where I begin.

BOBBY KENNEDY

One of the first larger-than-life figures I interviewed was Hubert Humphrey in 1976. At the time, he was the former vice president and considering a comeback run for president. But I joke that Bobby Kennedy was my first interview. He was coming to Elmira, New York, when running for the Senate. His motorcade was to go down College Avenue, which was right at the top of my street. My friend Tom DeMott and I rode our bicycles up to the parade route, and after Kennedy went by in an open-air convertible we started following it, side by side, along the route. We kept saying, "Hey Bobby." He glanced at us and said, "Hello, boys." Then he turned to a member of his security detail and said, "Get those kids out of here." We dropped back but continued to his speech location at the Mark Twain Hotel. Afterward, we shook his hand as he walked down the stairs to leave the place.

HILLARY IN OHIO—WHAT WENT WRONG

During the presidential campaign of 2016 I was having a hard time getting anyone from Hillary's campaign to come on camera and speak for her. The one person they did provide was Joseph Kennedy III, a congressman from Massachusetts, and the great-grandson of Bobby Kennedy. We did an interview about his support for Hillary Clinton, and at the end, I told him jokingly about the "interview" I had done with his grandfather. He laughed, and then said, "I'm sorry." I said, "Are you kidding? I've been telling that story and getting laughs for decades."

In my view the Democrats, by making only Congressman Kennedy available to local media, represented the very stark difference between how the Clinton campaign viewed Ohio and how the Trump campaign did. I tried and tried to reach people on Hillary's side. No luck. The reason I tried so hard was to be fair. The Republicans gave me all kinds of big names: Donald Trump, twice; Rudy Giuliani; Eric Trump; and Donald Trump Jr.

Donald Trump Jr. was an avid outdoorsman and we caught up with him at an outdoor hunting, camping, and fishing store in Ashland. We did an interview and he toured the store and met people. At the end, he was speaking to a crowd that had gathered. I was kneeling in front with my microphone because I didn't want to block anyone's view. He was in his last couple of words when my phone rang. I had forgotten to silence it. I looked down, stopped the ringing, and looked up. "It's my wife," I said.

Without a pause he said, "Would you like me to speak to her?" The crowd heard him say it and cheered. I answered the phone and said, "Hey, do you want to talk to Donald Trump Jr.?" Kim said, "What?" I handed him the phone and he said, "Hello, Kim, this is Donald Trump Jr." He was quick on his feet because I hadn't said her name, but he saw it on my screen and knew what to do. The crowd loved it!

What he said to her next played well with the crowd, too. "Your husband is a reporter. You know, reporters haven't been too kind to us." She was a gem. "Oh, he's not like the rest of them," Kim responded. "He's always fair." He looked at the crowd and said, "I think we're making some news here." He thanked her and said, "Nice speaking to you," and the crowd roared again. We all had a good laugh!

That's the kind of opportunity I think the Clinton campaign missed in 2016 in states like Ohio, Wisconsin, and Pennsylvania. The campaign took the Midwest for granted and had the states snatched out from under them. It is my opinion and nothing more, but in my mind, a candidate or one of their surrogates fares much better in any city when they speak to a trusted local reporter. Anyone can get a soundbite from the network or one provided by the campaign. But the local feel is missing.

REAGAN

I didn't interview Ronald Reagan, but I did cover one of his whistle-stop tours in Miamisburg, Ohio. It was intended to be reminiscent of a Herbert Hoover–style event as he went through three or four western Ohio cities by train. He stopped in each city and spoke from the back of the last car on the train. All I can say is that his nickname "The Great Communicator" was well deserved. He knew exactly how to win over a crowd. After he was elected president, I had a taste of the same ability at his stop at the Timken Steel plant in Canton. The Timken family was staunchly Republican, and they invited the president there to cut the ribbon on a huge new facility. From the way Reagan spoke, you would have thought he and Tim Timken had built the place together by hand. It was no brag, just his way of turning a phrase to warm up to workers who had a new lease on their jobs. It had another effect—either raising their boss to the status of a president or bringing the presidency down to a level that they could connect with. Reagan got it!

MCCAIN AND PALIN

John McCain's campaign lacked luster and was, in my view, a long shot from the very start against that of Barack Obama. Make no mistake, McCain was a great American on many well-publicized levels. I saw him a couple of times and interviewed him once. He had an admirable passion for this country, but politically, no spark.

I often wonder if his selection of Sarah Palin hurt him. She was a surprise to everyone and generated a lot of initial interest, but it faded as more was learned about her. Was she ready to be vice president of the United States? I don't have an answer, but the voters spoke.

I covered Palin and interviewed her at one of those "spontaneous" stops all candidates make at morning coffee shops or diners. Reporters usually get about a half-hour notice once the Secret Service clears the place. In this case, it was Karl's deli on West Third Street in Cleveland. Palin went into the deli, and only the network pool cameras were allowed in. When she came out, we did an interview with her, and she left. She seemed nice enough. My next move got me a bit of criticism. After she left, I went into Karl's. I know Karl and asked, "Where did she sit?" Karl pointed to a booth that a waitress was just clearing. I asked her if she would hold on a minute. "Karl, which one was her plate?" I asked. He told me. "Is that her half-eaten corned beef sandwich?" Yes, he said. I used it in my stand-up. Some folks didn't like it—they thought I was being too intrusive. Hey, after all, they hadn't let us local TV folks inside, and I was just trying to make a routine campaign ritual a little less routine!

OBAMA BUS TOUR

Probably the most up-close and insightful look I got at a candidate was when Barack Obama ran for and won his first term as president. He was doing a bus tour of Southern Ohio. Marty and I were assigned to ride the campaign bus with him for a couple of days. We flew to Dayton to meet up with the campaign. The first stop was at the Dayton Dragons Class A baseball stadium. It was a warm day. Obama began to speak, and at one point, he took off his coat. A few minutes later he rolled up his sleeves as if to send a message of *Let's get to work.*

Next, back on to the bus and a ride to Cincinnati for another stop. There, Marty and I noticed something. Again, Obama at one point took off his coat and later rolled up his sleeves. I took note of where he was in the speech when he did this. Back onto the bus for the final stop of the day, Portsmouth, and another speech. There I saw I was onto something. The coat came off at about the same time as the Cincinnati speech, and the same with the sleeves being rolled up. I can't say it was planned, but intended or not, his crowds got his message.

I almost forgot that on the way to one of the events there was one of those spontaneous "unplanned" stops at a diner. He went in and got a piece of coconut cream pie (as I recall), had a bite or two, shook some hands, and started back toward our bus. I was walking alongside of him when he suddenly turned to move toward the crowd. They were yelling his name. By his turning that way, I was now in the way of him having a clear path back to the bus. I felt a firm tug on my arm. It was enough to get me out of the way. The Secret Service agent told me later that they can never have anything in the way of a candidate making it back to the bus for shelter in case of trouble. I watched them the rest of the trip and saw it was true.

I enjoyed being with the national media. At typical campaign rallies I had covered in the past, after the photographer set up his equipment in the venue, we both were kicked out for a couple of hours while the equipment and the entire venue was searched. There was always a lot of standing around and waiting. We were allowed back inside after going through metal detectors a second time and waiting for another couple of hours.

We always knew it was getting close to showtime when the

national media came in and went to the spots reserved for them—always in front of where we had been assigned. They never went through screening. I had hoped one day to see how that felt. This time, I was in that position.

We were up and ready to leave at 7 a.m. from our hotel in Portsmouth. We dropped off our gear at the Obama bus, went to eat breakfast, and relaxed. The gear was being screened while we ate. We got on the bus afterward and had to wait for an hour while Obama worked out. It was well worth the wait when we arrived at the next stop. For the second day in a row, I could just walk in front of all those local cameras. How did it feel? Great!

On to Chillicothe as we headed north. The speech was pretty much the same. Any presidential candidate's campaign speech includes the names of local politicians, a few big donors, and one or two local issues. This is usually followed by the candidate's national agenda. As predicted, Obama's coat came off and the sleeves rolled up. I joked with Marty that I wish I had remembered which sleeve was rolled up first and if it was the same one every time. Columbus was our final stop. It was the same story as the others. After that, Obama was leaving the state, so we rented a car and drove home to Cleveland.

THE REPUBLICAN NATIONAL CONVENTION IN CLEVELAND

THE RUMOR WAS OUT THERE. The Republican Party was looking for a place to hold its 2016 national convention, and Cleveland wanted it. The convention would be a bonanza worth millions of dollars to the city that won the bid. It would also take a lot of up-front money from any city that placed a bid. And it would take planning on a scale that was hard to imagine. Yes, it would be followed by a huge federal grant, but the losing cities wouldn't get that—after having invested millions in research, collaboration, and even the start of infrastructure planning. Still, Cleveland wanted it, and wanted it bad.

The city planned and did all the necessary legwork. Their secrecy was frustrating to those of us in the media—and I believe at times it was in violation of sunshine laws. I battled them on it but lost that fight. But as a result of all that work, Cleveland won its bid to host the convention.

Cleveland won! I have no doubt that the rest of the nation was shocked. What the rest of the country didn't know, and the city had demonstrated to the advance teams scouting possible locations, is that slowly and surely Cleveland had built hotel after hotel. This included a nearly completed forty-two-story Hilton and a newly opened, million-square-foot convention center. The downtown population, once at less than 5,000, was now well over 16,000. People were moving into condo and apartment conversions of long-abandoned downtown buildings that were now generating tax revenue and jobs. Most of these were younger people who wanted to be close to work, many taking bikes to work, some not even owning cars—living, eating, getting groceries, and recreating downtown. That led to a more vibrant nightlife and a city that was always walkable now being even more walkable, and with more places to walk to. I don't mean to sugar-coat it—things weren't perfect (even today, retail is sadly lacking downtown)—but downtown Cleveland was a lot different from what out-of-towners were expecting.

I got a call just a few hours before the convention location decision was to be announced. I learned that Reince Priebus, the Republican Party chairman, would announce the winning city on Fox News at 11 a.m. I had good sources—people I had worked with for months in Governor John Kasich's office on this issue. They had told me weeks before that they would get only five to ten minutes' advance notice of the announcement of the winning city. They didn't know what day it would come. Now the time was here to find out.

I called a couple of my Kasich people that morning, and they said again that they wouldn't know until five minutes ahead of the announcement. In the newsroom, our eyes were trained on Fox News. Fox teased that Priebus was coming up after the commercial break. While the commercials ran, my cell phone rang. A terse message came, "It's Cleveland." I said, "Can I go with it?" The source said, "It's Cleveland."

I yelled across the newsroom to news director Dan Salamone. "Dan, it's Cleveland." Dan always trusted me. He didn't blink an eye and told our website people, who had a story prepared, "Go with it." He told the TV people ready to do an on-air cut-in to go with it, too. They did. We beat the RNC's announcement on Fox by four minutes!

Something the size of a major party's national political convention coming to Cleveland had been unimaginable to me. Now, the city and a thousand media outlets began to make plans. I'm not kidding—a thousand media outlets! It would require more digital bandwidth than ten cities could handle. Then there would be the matter of finding a space with enough room to house the inflated egos of that many reporters. But I digress!

Where to house the media outlets, where to hold the actual convention, where to house the delegates . . . it was a huge logistical challenge for everyone. But throughout it all, a kind of *esprit de corps*—"We are Cleveland, everyone else can go to hell!"—emerged. It was infectious. "We will do this," was a rallying cry.

But doing it was a lot of work. And a lot of money.

I will spare you details of my confrontations with the city over all those hidden meetings because our disagreements on that issue were never resolved by a court. Millions of tax dollars were being spent, some of them local and about $95 million from a federal grant. I understand the need to keep security details in confidence, but the public got no word on how their money was spent. Finding out was my job, but the city's roadblocks stopped me from fully doing it. Still ticks me off! Eventually, about a year after the convention, we finally got the information.

But we knew at the time that it was a huge endeavor. Quicken Loans Arena was chosen to be the venue for the actual delegates and speeches.

A parking garage next to the arena had to be turned into an office building for the media. That meant no parking there for weeks, for anyone. I was amazed that it was only weeks, not months. When I first walked into the parking garage after the makeover, I was shocked. It pretty much looked like an office except for the slowly rising floors as you went up level to level. It got done!

Digital bandwidth was another hurdle. Clearly, none of this was provided to any media outlet for free. I don't know what it cost an individual station, but I'm sure it was plenty. I know that just to get Wi-Fi service from AT&T (a convention sponsor) for the convention in the arena was $10,000 per media outlet. With that much bandwidth being used, it was essential to buy Wi-Fi access to get a signal out of the arena. AT&T brought in portable Wi-Fi generators that were seen all over the city to satisfy the demand. It got done!

The luxury boxes were even more highly priced. I don't know

the numbers, but I know that all the furniture from the existing luxury boxes at the arena was removed. Sheetrock and new walls were put over existing walls for easy removal afterward. If you wanted to rent a luxury box for your anchor team, there was a catalogue from one and only one company from which to choose furniture—anchor desk, director chairs, and so on. Location was another price consideration. Side view, front view, or the cheaper back of the podium view? I was down on the floor with the delegates for the actual convention and nomination, so none of that mattered to me. But hearing the stories about it amazed me. It got done!

A convention is, largely, a staged event. There was a committee meeting the first day that would have opened the nomination to anyone. It was clearly going to be defeated. Donald Trump was the obvious nominee as a result of the primary elections and caucuses. Now the anticipation was: What would Trump do when he made an appearance?

We in the media had to obtain credentials weeks in advance. Mine were the hardest to get because I would be on the floor of the convention within feet of anyone I wanted to talk to.

I filled out the forms, which asked all kinds of things, including a lot of very personal questions. Date of birth, obviously. Where I was born. Copy of my driver's license, a second photo of me, passport, mother's maiden name, had I ever been arrested? That last one puzzled me. I thought they should be able to figure that out themselves. I suppose they were looking to see if anyone lied about their past.

A few weeks later, several credentials arrived. One allowed me to be inside the blocks-wide perimeter, which was encircled by a ten-foot-high fence. One of the walls ran down the middle of Euclid Avenue, a main corridor during rush hour, cutting the street in half. Another credential got me closer. The final credential got me into the arena—but only after going through a large tent where everyone covering the event passed through metal detectors along with their equipment. Very long lines.

On the second day, walking to the arena with Marty, I passed the convention center, about a half-mile from the floor of the arena. I noticed a man sitting behind a small table. He was wearing a suit and tie, looking very official. I didn't think much about it. At the table, he had a computer and screen that beeped when I walked past it. Later I wondered, *What was that?* The next day we walked the same route, and after passing the table I turned to look at the computer monitor. There was my picture, all my personal information, who I worked for, and my level of credentialing. I hadn't been stopped, scanned, screened, or gone through a metal detector. Turns out that the highest-level credential I was wearing around my neck, provided by the Secret Service, had a chip in it. I am told there were facial recognition features as well. When I walked by the scanner, they knew exactly who I was without any contact with me whatsoever.

I had no problem with this level of security in that scenario. Now, although I don't know if Big Brother is watching, I know he can if he wants to!

This whole convention was going to be a show, that was clear. The night before the nomination, the night Melania was to speak, we got a preview of the event's video treatment—lighting, sound, and everything. The Donald's people knew what they were doing. It was going to be a spectacle.

It was customary for the presidential nominee not to appear at the convention before the night he was nominated. But this was Donald Trump. As Melania ended her talk, the curtains opened, and out came Donald. The crowd went wild. He knew who he was talking to, and it sure seemed that he didn't care about anything but pleasing them.

For news media, there was a lot of standing around and waiting associated with the convention. I think people have an idea of reporters running here and there and a lot of excitement. Sometimes that was true, but another side of the story was having to walk a mile or a mile-and-a-half to the site to get around, and eventually through, all the fencing. There was a clear lack of parking nearby, so that meant also carrying many pounds of equipment. My camera-man was Marty DeChant. After we cleared the security tents with hundreds of other reporters, we had little to do from noon to about 7 p.m. except for trying to spot something or someone of note to video or interview for use later. After the night's events, we'd have to retrace our route back to the TV station at about one or two in the morning. I know, "Boo-hoo to you, Paul." By the way, I did have a hip replacement two years later. Unrelated.

Trump was a dynamic speaker but, let's be honest, he was talking to party loyalists. What did you expect? I don't think I need to say a lot about the speech or the reaction, as it was pre-dictable. One moment was not so predictable. Texas Senator Ted Cruz came to the stage. The drama was intense. Would he endorse his former foe for the nomination or not? He gave a speech that didn't give you a clue. Then at the end came the cliffhanger. The crowd was waiting, even urging him get on board with Trump. He didn't endorse Trump. He didn't say he didn't. He just left the question open. There was a pause, then the crowd let out a large and extended boo. It was deafening from the floor. I was less than twenty-five yards away. Later I watched the networks' coverage of it. The coverage bore no resemblance to what I heard from the floor that night. I'm not sure if it was bad microphone placement or something else. But I was there. It was deafening!

I think a lot of the national media were stuck on that original headline of "Cleveland?" A story after the convention in the *Washington Post* summed it up best: "We were promised a riot. In Cleve-land, we got a block party instead."

It didn't come easy, but it got done.

WITNESSING AN EXECUTION: FRANK SPISAK

ONE OF THE MOST MEMORABLE characters I ever encountered was Frank Spisak. I was a witness to his execution.

The story began in February of 1982 with the murder of Rev. Horace Rickerson, a Black man, in a bathroom at Cleveland State University. Several months later, John Hardaway, another Black man, was shot seven times at the West 117th Street rapid station. Hardaway survived. Then a female employee at Cleveland State was forced into a bathroom stall by a man. She pushed him away and ran; he fired and missed.

We reporters were wondering about this connection to Cleveland State. WEWS, where I worked at the time, was located just a couple of blocks from the Cleveland State campus. All of us working there became extremely cautious when exiting the building after the 11 p.m. news.

The violence continued.

Timothy Sheehan was the next victim, also shot in a restroom at Cleveland State. A maintenance supervisor at the university, Sheehan was white.

Days later, Brian Warford, a student at CSU who was Black, was shot and killed at a bus stop close to WEWS.

Fear was spreading, not only in the newsroom, but throughout the city.

It took months to identify and arrest the perpetrator. When it happened, it was his own doing. He had been arrested for firing a gun out of a window at his apartment. After he was arrested and released on bond, a tip to police said they should check the gun. They did, and got a match to one of the recent killings.

And Frank Spisak was arrested for murder.

Spisak, it turned out, was a cross-dresser who often went by the name Francine. He was also an avowed Nazi who wore a Hitler-style moustache. I had a source in the police department who gave me some background and Spisak's address. I went there with a cameraman the day he was arrested. Spisak's wife came to the door. I asked her about what the police source had told me. It was uncomfortable. "Did Frank ever dress up in women's clothing?" The answer was yes. "Did he ever bring men home and ask you to sleep on the couch while they used the bedroom?" The answer was yes. On and on it went. One question sticks with me. I asked if he played Nazi marches on the stereo. She said yes, then, staring vaguely at me, said, "But he liked all kinds of music—disco, polkas. He always said he'd take me to *Polka Varieties* one day." *Polka Varieties* was a long-running show that aired on WEWS each week. It was an almost surreal interview.

At trial, Spisak entered a plea of not guilty by reason of insanity, claiming his actions were taken due to direct orders from God. The courtroom was a circus. At one point, Spisak addressed the court, saying, "I have lived for the Aryan Nation, and after my death I shall revive in the spirit of those who chose to follow my example. Heil Hitler!"

Getting a first look at Spisak in court almost took my breath away. The Hitler moustache was his most pronounced feature. He had Coke-bottle glasses and often used the "Sieg Heil" salute with his arm outstretched with an open palm. Chilling.

Spisak was convicted and sentenced to death.

There were seemingly endless appeals, which took many years. But finally, in 2011, the clock stopped ticking for Frank Spisak.

I was the designated TV reporter for his execution. At executions, there are always media witnesses from the home city where a crime happened. One from radio, one from TV, and one from a newspaper.

I was chosen because I was the last reporter standing who had covered the trial, twenty-nine years earlier. As the execution got closer, I had a question: As a Catholic, was I doing something wrong?

Fortunately, I had a great way to find out. My wife, Kim, and I had become good friends with Cleveland Bishop Richard Lennon. The year before, he had asked us to co-chair the Catholic Charities Annual Appeal. I went to the Cathedral one day, and after Mass asked him straight out: "Should I be doing this?" His words were comforting. He said that I wasn't doing anything wrong. "As Catholics we obey the laws of the nation, and we work to change the laws that Catholic doctrine is in conflict with." He told me that it is no different from a judge or juror in a murder case. If the law called for the death penalty, then that was a civic responsibility, but working to change the law remained Catholic teaching.

We arrived at the Lucasville prison, about four-and-a-half hours south of Cleveland, and went through security. It is always odd, as you pass through locked door after locked door, to hear the prior one clang shut behind you.

We waited in a holding area until a few minutes before the execution. We were given briefings every hour or so: How he slept, if he had any visitors, even what he requested for his final meal. It was spaghetti with tomato sauce, a salad, chocolate cake, and coffee.

It seemed like days, but eventually the call came for the witnesses to follow a guard to another room. There, we were told what to expect, the protocol to be followed, what drugs were being used, and that he might even snore after administration of the drugs. It was a three-drug combination. One renders the condemned unconscious, another stops his breathing, and one stops the heart. At last it was time to go across a courtyard into another building known as the "death house." My heart was pounding.

We walked in, turned to our right, and went into a room with two rows of seats facing a glass window that looked directly into the death chamber. A gurney was there with several tie-down straps and officers waiting to do their assigned jobs. On a TV monitor, we could see that Spisak was in another room where shunts were being put into his arms to make for a faster connection once he was led to the death chamber. Soon he came in, his arms outstretched due to supports at his elbows so that the shunts wouldn't be dislodged.

Spisak stepped onto a small stool, aided by officers, lay down, and was strapped in. It happened with razor-sharp precision. Clearly, the officers had trained repeatedly for this. I noted that throughout the entire process, each step seemed designed to keep the inmate from agitation. I would be going too far to say it was compassionate, but clearly much thought had been given to the condemned and his family.

With Spisak strapped down, Warden Donald Morgan read the death warrant from the Ohio Supreme Court, authorizing the execution. Next, he asked if Spisak wanted to make a final statement. He did.

The warden took the statement Spisak had written out of his jacket pocket, unfolded it, and placed it in front of Spisak's face. Spisak began to read it, in German, using a Hitler-like cadence. It was shocking! What happened next was just odd.

Spisak stopped reading, and in a very calm voice asked the warden if he would adjust the paper saying, "Can you move that back? It's a little blurry." The warden did, and Spisak began reading in German again but only for a couple of words. He politely said, "Can you move it a little more." The warden obliged, Spisak thanked him and he read the rest with the Hitler cadence in German.

We were given a translation of his final statement by the Department of Corrections. He had read from the book of Revelations—passages dealing with the end of the world, Christ's return, and everyone eventually going to heaven. He had stopped before getting to the part of Revelations where it refers to the abominable, murderers and liars burning with fire and brimstone. His last words were, "Heil Herr!" We were told at the time, it translated to "Praise God!" but I later learned that *Herr* means "mister" in German.

When Spisak finished reading, the warden stepped back and

buttoned his jacket. That was the signal for the flow of chemicals to begin. I saw no reaction from Spisak, just shallow breathing, and then no breathing. It seemed to me that he was gone in about three minutes. In about ten minutes all the fluid had been administered, and a curtain was pulled over the window. This is the time when a doctor examines the inmate and pronounces him dead. The curtain is to protect the identity of the physician. In short order, the curtain opened, and the warden announced the time of death. John Hardaway, whom Spisak had shot twenty-nine years before, was in the room. He said nothing. I sat next to Cathy, a daughter of Timothy Sheehan.

My duty after the execution was to face the cameras and report on what I had seen for all the TV stations in Ohio. I thought I did a fairly good job. The next day we drove back to Cleveland and I watched a tape of my briefing. I looked like a deer in the head-lights—not the concise, insightful observations I thought I had delivered. Clearly, the experience had a profound impact on me. It is an experience I will never forget.

An interesting aside to the story is that Sheehan was killed on his son Brendan's fifteenth birthday. I met Brendan briefly at the trial. He went to law school and for a time was a law clerk in Federal Judge Donald Nugent's court. Nugent prosecuted the Spisak case and had taken Brendan under his wing ever since. Brendan later became an assistant county prosecutor and today is the Presiding and Administrative Judge for the Cuyahoga County Common Pleas Court. He is also a true and loyal friend of mine.

ADVENTURES ABOVE
AND BELOW GROUND

GROWING UP WHEN I DID, I have always been a fan of flight. I watched every NASA space launch—Mercury, Gemini, Apollo, and beyond. In those days, for many families a Sunday afternoon after church and Sunday dinner might include a trip to the airport to watch a couple of planes come in (and if all the kids behaved, maybe an ice cream cone after). Later, my career in television news gave me opportunities to explore that fascination as I covered stories related to NASA and other aeronautical topics. News stories also took me deep underground, which I also found fascinating. Here are a few of those adventures . . .

THUNDERBIRDS

I once flew on the Concorde, the supersonic commercial airliner. We were doing a story on British Airways initiating a flight from Cleveland to Europe. The flight itself was unremarkable. Cameraman Dave Hollis and I flew from Cleveland to New York, so we didn't actually reach supersonic speeds (which were restricted over land). The main thing that hit me was that the plane was a very narrow tube, just two seats on each side of the aisle, and it felt very constricted. Dave got to be in the cockpit, so he probably had the more interesting ride.

Flying with the U.S. Air Force Thunderbirds was quite the opposite. The Thunderbirds would be featured at the annual Cleveland National Air Show over Labor Day weekend, and to help publicize the event they would take a few reporters up for a joy ride. This year was my turn.

At Burke Lakefront Airport, I received a briefing from a flight team member. Then I climbed into the fighter jet. From the second we took off, I knew that this was no everyday flight. The acceleration was unbelievable! Not a feeling of being pushed back in your seat as you took off—rather, I felt it on my rear end because even while appearing to ascend only slowly, we were climbing very high and very fast, nose forward.

After we were airborne, the pilot told me over the headset exactly what we would be doing. He would do several maneuvers, tell me what he did with the controls to execute each one, and then let me try it. I was seated behind him with my own set of controls.

As we began the first maneuver, he said, "Paul, I'm going to execute a series of snap rolls at one-second intervals. Are you ready?" I said "Sure," and the word was hardly out of my mouth when the earth that had been below me was suddenly on my left. A second later it was above me—I was upside down. Then to the right, and finally back to where it belonged. The pilot then told me how to do it. Then, as you might imagine, I failed miserably at doing it myself.

We performed a few other maneuvers, which I also couldn't do. The pilot's skill was amazing! At one point, he said that we were going to do a full, over-the-top, backward roll to experience G-forces. As we climbed at the start of what would be the loop, he called out the numbers. "Paul, that is two Gs, now three, we are at four, five, and six." I don't know how many there were. The skin on my face was pulled back freakishly. Suddenly he leveled out and we were weightless for a moment. It was cool—but my stomach didn't think so. It began churning. But I held it together.

We headed back toward the airport. It was a cloudy day, so we couldn't see the ground. We got close and the pilot said, "Paul, that concludes our demonstration ride, would you like to see the way we take a jet from 22,000 feet down to 2,000 feet?" "Sure." He flipped it over backward as he had done before, and we headed straight down. After a few seconds, he punched through the cloud cover, and there was Lake Erie below us—but coming at us, fast! Then, we leveled out, and there was Burke Airport in front of us. He knew exactly where he was. I did too, physically.

I hit the button on the stick to talk and said, "That did it for me." He almost sounded pleased when he said, "It's on your right." In a pocket in the cockpit next to me was a barf bag. I used it. As we were just about to touch the ground, he said, "I'll pop the shroud when we land, and you'll feel better." We landed, I got some fresh air, and was fine. However, my camera crew taping the story never let me forget it. As usual, my embarrassment was my own doing: When we pulled up to the gate, I stupidly held up the barf bag. Mistake. They showed it to everyone at the station for a laugh, of course. I couldn't deny it. But that ride was a thrill I will never forget!

THE VOMIT COMET

NASA's weightless test plane, which was nicknamed "The Vomit Comet," was based at the NASA Lewis (now NASA Glenn) research facility in Cleveland near Hopkins Airport. I did some checking and found that I could get a demonstration ride. They wouldn't do it just for me, but the next time they were taking an experiment up on the plane, I could go along. The call came several weeks later.

Cameraman "Cowboy" Joe Butano and I went to the NASA facility, and after clearing rigid security we were led to a building where we met the pilot and co-pilot. They explained that we would be weightless for about twenty seconds. It's not a straight dive downward. The plane is actually climbing at negative air speed for ten seconds, which passengers experience as weightlessness; then, as it hits the top of the parabola, you experience weightlessness for another ten seconds on the way down.

First, we flew south to restricted air space near Wright-Patterson Air Force Base near Dayton. We got there in a snap. I don't know the speed, but I can tell you that we could feel it. We got to Mansfield, an hour's drive or more south of Cleveland, in six minutes.

Joe was a real character and a fun guy to work with. The pilot told us that we had enough fuel to do five dives. Joe and I had to plan. I clearly wanted to do something where I would float, and where I could show the microphone floating. We had five shots to get it right. After we did three dives, Joe, an Italian American with olive-colored skin, already was looking almost green. He had about had it. "Joe, can we do one more?" I asked. He he agreed.

After the fourth dive, Joe was done. There was no fifth dive. I don't want to sound macho, though—had we done that fifth dive, I would have gotten sick!

THE GOODYEAR BLIMP

Quite unlike the Vomit Comet, the Goodyear Blimp is the most pleasant ride you can ever experience. That is, once you get up into the air. I learned that the most dangerous points in the ride are the takeoff and landing, when the blimp is closest to the ground and the most susceptible to winds.

When we got on, the blimp was held down by crew members holding ropes. We were urged to get on quickly. Then the blimp took off. Not a floating, gently majestic kind of takeoff that you might imagine: it was nose up, quickly, to get away from the ground.

Cameraman Rich Geyser and I were doing a live shot from the blimp, which was in town to cover *Monday Night Football*. We had another camera in our helicopter shooting us from a distance.

The blimps are built in Akron, home of Goodyear, and there is usually one stationed at the hanger in Akron, so we see them around a lot. But being on it was special.

Getting off the blimp was the same deal: It came down in a hurry, crew members grabbed the ropes, and we were escorted off quickly. At the time, the passenger compartment could hold about eight passengers. (The compartment was later enlarged.) The pilot used a big wheel and pedals to control it. (No doubt more computers are involved these days.)

That flight took me back to a boyhood fantasy. In upstate New

York, we would see the blimp once every October when the Grand Prix of the United States was held in Watkins Glen, about twenty miles from my parents' home. Each year I would see it and wonder how cool it would be to be on it. I was lucky to find out, and I wasn't disappointed.

A BAD HELICOPTER RIDE

I was done with helicopters after this one. A commercial commuter plane crashed in Orchard Park, near Buffalo, and CBS wanted footage from the air. Cameraman Dan "Wags" Wagner and I were dispatched to get it. Problem was, the same storm that had contributed to the crash was now headed our way. It was treetop flying almost immediately, with the pilot telling us to watch for high-tension electric lines. We flew through squall after squall. No fun. We decided to land in Ashtabula, where we waited a couple of hours for the weather to clear before moving on to Jamestown, New York, for fuel and then on to Orchard Park. We got the video, returned to Jamestown to refuel, got back in the air, and we finally got close enough to Cleveland that we sent our footage via microwave from the chopper to the station. They uplinked it to CBS by satellite. That was a nightmare ride. I have never been on a helicopter since, and don't intend to get on one!

ASTRONAUT

When I was a child, astronauts were national heroes—those men remembered in the book and movie *The Right Stuff.*

Later, when I was a working in TV news, astronauts became a more diverse group of people and were no less heroic. But some of them also became real people to me because I got to meet them when covering them for stories.

Astronaut Bob Overmyer was from Northeast Ohio. An Air Force colonel, he was chosen to be second in command on NASA's Shuttle STS-5 mission, the fifth in the space shuttle program. I knew that he was from Westlake, where we lived at the time, and as a younger guy was a good high school athlete who worked summers at Dean's Greenhouse, not far from my home. In his astronaut publicity photo, he was a stern-looking guy with a military flat-top. Although smiling in the photo, you could tell he was a no-nonsense man.

I set up a trip to NASA in Houston to interview him. What a surprise it was! We waited with a PR person outside a government building to meet him. Bob came around the corner in a red sports car at a pretty good clip. "It's boring here," he said. "Let's do it at my house." We followed him, met his family, and did the interview. A delightful guy. Later, I talked to Dolly Dean at the greenhouse back in Westlake, and she wasn't surprised about where Bob wound up. Bob was a thrill-seeker, she said.

I went to Florida for the launch of Bob's mission. I had my background stories about Bob already finished, waiting to be aired on TV in Cleveland. I was in Florida for a live intro to the stories and to report on the launch the next day. The night before launch, cameraman Tom Livingston and I were trying to figure out where to do our story. Tom was vacationing there and had his conversion van. We planned to camp out at the Cape, sleep in his van, and be on site first thing in the morning for the launch.

CNN had a trailer there with a news anchor desk. Nothing fancy. They weren't using it, and our station had a relationship with them, so we were allowed to use it for our story. That made it look like we had planned way better than we really had. One problem. I introduced the story, and then back in Cleveland the station ran the story intended for the *next* night. So while STS-5 sat on the launch pad and the crew was likely sleeping in the nearby crew quarters, my previously recorded story that began, "Now that the astronauts are in orbit . . ." Not a good way to start. The only actual launch was my emotions—into a tirade! Tom was more levelheaded than I was. "Let's get a beer," was all he said.

The next day, the real launch went well.

Later, Bob came to Cleveland for a post-flight publicity tour. I met him at Hopkins Airport to get a quick interview. As we walked down to baggage claim, I asked him, "What was it like?" He said, "To be honest with you, at the point of maximum dynamic pressure during launch, I thought the damn thing was going to break up." Rare insight into the anxieties even the bravest of our pioneers face in pushing science forward.

Bob later was commander on another shuttle mission. He retired from NASA and worked as a test pilot for private companies. Sadly, in 1996 Bob was killed in Duluth, Minnesota, when an experimental plane he was testing for stall recovery characteristics crashed. He is buried at Arlington National Cemetery.

*   *   *

I got word from the assignment desk that Jim Lovell, the commander of Apollo 13, was coming to an elementary school in Parma. He attended the school before his family moved away. I insisted to our news director that I cover his visit. It wasn't a big story—they dedicated a playground in his name. I didn't care; I just wanted to meet him. At the beginning of the interview, I told Lovell that I had a question I'd ask at the end that he'd never been asked before. He chuckled. "I think I've been asked every question imaginable, so we'll find out."

I did the interview about the playground and his youth in Parma. When it ended, Lovell wanted to hear what my last question was. "Did you guys really like Tang?" I asked. He laughed. "You're right; I've never been asked that question." The answer? "We preferred another company's orange drink because it had pulp." NASA, however, chose Tang.

THE B-24 LIBERATOR

Like so many who served in World War II, my dad didn't like to talk much about the war. He was a navigator on a heavy bomber, the B-24 Liberator, during the war. It was a big, slow aircraft that had a horrible rate of being shot down and crews dying. He was in the European theater. His unit was based in North Africa and later Italy. They did bomb runs over oil fields and factories in Germany and many other countries.

I would ask about the war, and he would mostly say, "It was a long time ago." Because of that, I didn't know much about what he did. He kept a journal of his flights, but only what targets they bombed and stuff like that. He was a man of few words. His entry in the journal the day the war ended was "Fini." You can't get much shorter than that.

There is just one B-24 left flying, and it was going to be at a suburban airport near Cleveland. I went there with cameraman Marty DeChant. To get on this bucket of bolts, we had to crawl up through the opening into which the front wheel would retract after the plane took off. That led to the cockpit. The navigator was down a level, with his instruments and the bomb sight. One thing was immediately crystal clear: If there was a problem or they were hit by enemy fire, there was almost no way the navigator—or any of the crew—could get out. It was a flying death trap!

My dad did tell me one story about his crew being able to survive above the normal fatality rate of the B-24. The plane always flew with fighters alongside to protect it. He said that they loved it when their protection came from a fighter group trained in Tuskegee. They were all Black and they were the very best, he said. The Tuskegee Airmen. He probably owed his life to them. And so do I: With no Joe Orlousky coming home from the war, there is no Paul Orlousky or any of my four siblings.

My dad died before I ever saw the Liberator. I met an old man who had served in the war with the Tuskegee Airmen. He lived in the apartments in the large building where our television studios were located. I told him a few times what my dad had said about their skill, and he got a broad smile each time. Now he is gone too.

THE SALT MINE

I can't tell you how many people have told me that they'd love to go down into the salt mines beneath Lake Erie. The entrance is near Edgewater Park on the West Side. I often said it, too. Then Bob Noll, an Emmy Award-winning producer at the station, made it happen. His father worked there.

When you get to the salt mine, they tell you that it is going to be dark and cold and that once you get to the bottom you will be going a couple of miles out under the lake. There, a vein of salt has been mined for decades. Estimates at the time of my visit said there was at least a hundred-year supply of road salt there.

The journey began with a slow elevator ride descending 1,756 feet below the surface—almost exactly one third of a mile.

After exiting the elevator, one of the first things I noticed was that the vehicles they were using were at least twenty years old—trucks I had seen on the street as a kid. These vehicles had been disassembled, lowered by elevator, and reassembled in the mine. There was a full-service garage to maintain them. "How do they last so long with all of this salt?" I wondered. Clearly my only experience with road salt was driving through it during the winter, and the salt eventually getting the better of my cars, leaving a lot of rust. The answer was that the air in the mine was kept at an extremely low humidity. I don't recall the temperature, but it was very cool.

As we rode on a vehicle resembling a heavy-duty golf cart deep into the mine, I had a weird feeling that if something went wrong, we were dead. We ventured on. The salt is cut out in blocks. We were told the pattern resembled a checkerboard with every other square (or cube, in this case) taken out. Where, exactly, we were under the lake above us, I have no idea. This was way before GPS (and I suppose down there GPS would not have worked, anyway).

The tour took us to the leading edge of the digging, where huge clawing machines chopped at the salt. The salt was then taken by truck back to the area near the elevator and placed on a constantly running conveyor belt that took it to the surface.

When the tour guide said it was time to go back to the elevator, I was relieved. It made me realize that I had an easy, relatively safe, well-paid job. It reminded me how many hard-working people of Cleveland do dangerous jobs for no recognition and average wages. I never forget it when I see a salt spreader during a winter storm. I still complain about the weather, but the workers who mine the salt make it easier to travel through it safely.

SEWER SPELUNKERS

We heard about a group of people who enjoyed exploring storm sewers around Greater Cleveland. There aren't a lot of caves in our area, so this was their chance to spelunk—a term I wasn't familiar with. We gave our story the working title "Sewer Spelunkers." We met our guides on a Sunday afternoon, and they outfitted cameraman Rich Geyser and me with some of the same gear you might use in exploring a cave. In we went. I don't know how much, if any, news value there was in the story—but it was fascinating.

Almost immediately, the resemblance to a cave was obvious. There were stalactites and stalagmites that had formed from decades of dripping water that was heavy with salt and calcium. In some cases, they resembled gems. There were also lots of cobwebs, various varmints, and even fish.

The leader called out where we were in the city, under this or that road. He assured us that he had checked the weather and there was no chance of rain. Until he said that, I had never thought that the pipes could become engorged with water during a heavy rain. This was a long time ago—I didn't think about safety back then nearly as much as I do now. I guess that's called common sense!

I loved doing the story but thought its news value was dubious. I also wondered, *Would other people go out and put themselves in danger because of the story?* This came at a time when TV news was changing, and now I learned something about those changes. Don Perris, the President of Scripps Howard Broadcasting, saw the advance promotion of the story, which by this time had a juiced-up title: "The Tunnels Time Forgot." I was in the promotion director's office as Perris pointed to a print ad for my story. "I want more of this," he said. Then, he pointed at an ad for a harder news story and said, "And less of that."

Don Perris was a genius in many ways. He was always ahead of the curve. Television was indeed changing.

TIPSTERS

YOU MAY HAVE NOTICED THAT I begin a lot of my stories with "I got a tip . . ." Investigative news stories aren't usually just dropped into your lap, though. A reporter must cultivate sources, and that takes time and trust.

During my time in the TV business, many reporters came and went. Most of those who came and went just took an assignment from the desk each day and headed out to make TV. Often, at the end of their first contract, they were headed to a smaller market.

The ones who came and *stayed* are ones who developed great sources. Carl Monday, Tom Meyer, Ed Gallek, Leon Bibb, Tom Beres, Bill Sheil, Ron Regan, Joe Pagonakis, and a handful of others.

Some reporters think it is a big deal to be on television, that when they arrive on a scene people should genuflect to them, that *they* are the story. Get over yourself. You, the reporter, are not the story. Reel yourself in. In fact, it pays to be approachable. When you talk to people like they were your next-door neighbor, you earn dividends. My best tipsters were people with whom I had just had a casual conversation, or people called because someone they knew had had that kind of a chat with me.

I mentioned trust. When a person comes to a reporter with a story, particularly one about their place of employment, they are understandably nervous. I tell them early on that their information is between the two of us. I never shared a source with anyone. Not news managers, not another reporter, and not my wife. That went a long way in gaining trust.

After the story aired, almost inevitably I'd get a call: "I think they know it's me. They're looking at me funny." With some hand-holding and reassurance, I'd calm the source down. "The only way they'll know," I'd tell them, "is if you act differently or tell them yourself." After a few days, their nerves would calm, and it would pass.

Some sources have watched too many movies about reporters and sources—*All the President's Men* comes to mind, and the scene with Woodward and Bernstein meeting a source in a parking garage during their Watergate investigation. People calling me would say, let's meet at this or that parking garage. I'd say, "No one knows why you're calling me. Just come in the front door and ask for me." (And to be honest, I wasn't going anywhere to meet someone I didn't know—I had been threatened enough times to know that wasn't smart.)

The best way to cultivate a source is to just be yourself, not some television news "personality." People I've met on the street and just listened to wind up being some of the best sources of stories. I might not have gotten anything for the news the day I spoke to them, and I might not have been looking for anything, but down the line it paid off a lot. We had a station softball team that I organized. I'd get calls years later from someone I'd played against who had a tip.

Police, security guards, and other people who see the comings and goings of public officials are like gold for a reporter seeking sources. But you can't just talk to them only when you're looking for information. Treat people with respect and show them you're just a regular guy. Two stories already mentioned come to mind, two of my biggest. The rescue of the three women who had been held captive by Ariel Castro for ten years, and the "Car 224, Where Are You?" story about police goofing off on the job. To this day, in each case, only the sources and I know who they are. People have tried to find out, particularly in the police case, but a promise of anonymity to a source is a bond never to be broken.

People sometimes are critical of reporters using anonymous sources. "Whoever called you just had an axe to grind," they say.

That statement is 100% true. Nobody called me about their friends. My bottom line, though, was whether the information they were giving me was true and if it had news value to either our viewers or to taxpayers. Many times, the stories exposed crimes.

Sometimes a viewer would call about a problem they were having with a business. I would say, "OK, we'll come out and talk to you." They'd say, "Oh, I don't want to go on television. I just want you to call them or go there and scare them." I'd laugh. I hope those who know me well don't see me as an ogre, the way some viewers did! Those calls always reminded me that from years of reporting on TV, I somehow had attained a certain kind of power in Northeast Ohio. That also came with a caution in my mind: *Use it wisely.*

Then there were the threats. Someone would call and say, "I'm gonna find you and kick your ass one of these days." My response was well rehearsed. "Good," I'd say, "because I am in a sh***y mood today. I got in a fight with my boss this morning, and it's been a lousy day at work—you're in for trouble, buddy." Then I'd slam the phone down. Usually, they would call back, saying they weren't kidding. My reply was also rehearsed, "Listen, I'm walking out the front door of the TV station at exactly 6:15. If you're there, I'm gonna kick your ass." I'd slam the phone down again. And later, at 6:15, I would leave the station—using the *side* door!

The threats never really bothered me. If someone is going to attack you, it will happen as you turn a street corner and get sucker punched. Threatening phone calls were just an attempt to scare me. The threat only worked if I let it.

COPS I'VE KNOWN
AND RESPECTED

A POLICE FUNERAL IS ALWAYS a tough story to cover for a news reporter. There is a tight blanket of security protecting the family, which is totally appropriate; but there is also the pomp and circumstance. The bagpipes, the military salutes, and the hearse driving past you. One time, standing outside the Cathedral of St. John the Evangelist, I was live, on-air, covering the funeral of Officer Jonathan Schroeder. We had been on the air for a while and the service ended. Just as the hearse passed me, our anchor, David Wittman, asked me a question. I was so choked up all I could say was, "David, I do have an answer but I can't really speak right now," as my voice cracked. That had never happened to me on the air before. That day, the sights, the sounds, and the gravity of the event got me.

THE ULTIMATE SACRIFICE

I think it would be strange to begin a story about my Cleveland Police Department heroes if I didn't begin with the names of those who died in the forty years I covered the streets of Northeast Ohio. The first was just weeks after I began working in Cleveland. The last was less than a year before I retired. I list their names separately because I don't want them to be bunched together. Each of their sacrifices made Cleveland safer. In all, more than one hundred officers have given their lives in the service to our great city. Seventy-five have died from gunfire.

Anthony Johnson Sr.
Benjamin Grair Jr.
Stephen Kovach
Ernest Holbert
Thomas Smith
Edward Claybrooks Jr.
Hilary Cudnik Sr.
Robert Clark II
David Smith
Wayne Leon
Jonathan Schroeder
Derek Owens
Marcia Figueroa
David Fahey Jr.

Most of the names immediately jump out at me, largely because I covered either their deaths or their funerals.

I'd also like to mention Grace Leon, wife of Wayne Leon, who became an outspoken champion for several causes including building a beautiful police memorial in Cleveland's West Park neighborhood. She was a heroine during a time of heartache when she was left with a young family. A shy person who never thought the spotlight would shine on her in such a tragic way. Her work in that spotlight has made a lot of people better.

SGT. ROGER DENNERLL

One of the most interesting police officers I ever met was Roger Dennerll. He was the sergeant in charge of the downtown Cleveland vice unit. The job included prostitution, drugs and occasionally gambling. The big shots in the department left him alone because he got results. I struck a fast friendship with Roger. I could call him at five in the afternoon on a slow news day and ask, "Roger, you got anything going tonight? We have a slow news day." He might say, "Just doing some hooker sweeps over on Lorain." If I was hard up for a story I'd ask, "Can we come along?" The answer was always yes.

From the back of the police car, the view of the world changes. I had seen Roger's unit bust many prostitutes. One day, I pointed out a woman who I thought might be working the streets and asked, "Roger, what about her?" In an instant, he said no. I asked how he knew. He had an answer that stuck with me. He said, "The prostitutes are walking, but they're not going anywhere."

At one point, I heard about a massage parlor that was rumored to be a house of prostitution. I tried to get someone in there to get an idea if it was true, but had no luck. I called Roger. He set up a sting and gave one of his guys some marked bills. His job was to try to get in while posing as a customer. The woman running the place was very sharp. She had a window that overlooked a muffler shop across the street on Superior Avenue. The shop had a pay phone outside. If you wanted to get in, she'd tell you to go there and call her when you got close. With her system, she could see if the caller was a person she recognized. In this case, she didn't recognize the detective, so we were out of options—I thought.

Roger had another idea. Cops would watch a customer go in and then, when he came out, stop him and see if they could get the guy to talk. A guy went in, and twenty minutes later he came out and got into his car. Two undercover police cars followed, and we followed them. About a mile later, they pulled him over. We had a microphone on Roger. He walked up to the driver and asked him get out of his car. "Sir, what was going on up there on Superior?" Roger asked. The guy flipped immediately and said, "I was at a house of prostitution." Roger repeated it because he wasn't sure if we could hear the guy. We could, but Roger repeating his every answer made it even funnier for me and cameraman Dave Hollis.

"And what did you do there?" Roger asked next. The answer, "I had sex." Back and forth it went, "You had sex with who?" "I had sex with a girl named Cindy." Just then, one of Roger's crew suggested that the guy take him into the place because the customer was well known there. "Sir," Roger asked, "would you be willing to take our undercover officer into the place and make an introduction?" Yes, the guy said, and Roger told him to wait right where he was. As Roger turned to talk to his crew, the man said, "But today wouldn't be good, I've got to get back to work." Roger's back stiffened and he turned on his heel saying, "Sir, let me explain to you what's going on here. Doin' it my way right here, like I just told you, is way easier than taking you to jail, towing your car and calling your wife. Can I say it any clearer to you sir?" Immediately the guy said, "Today would be fine."

The customer returned to the phone booth across the street from the massage parlor and asked to get back in. We were around the corner with the other cops. They charged into the place when the customer was let in and we followed, cameras rolling.

Inside, we found a guy who covered himself with a sheet immediately. Roger asked him, "What is going on here?" The guy said nothing. "Sir we just started doin' this job yesterday so I'm gonna believe you, okay?" Roger replied. "And if you tell me the Easter Bunny is comin' tomorrow, I'm gonna believe that too, okay? But we didn't just start doin' this job yesterday, so I think something is going on, and you're under arrest."

Cops and Reporters

The relationship between the police department and the media changed over the years. When George Forbes, then city council president, was a candidate for mayor, he announced a big crackdown on drugs in the King Kennedy public housing complex. We in the news media were given extensive access because he wanted the coverage to show how effective a leader he'd be. Drug boys were lined up against fences by detectives and searched. All kinds of drugs were found. Yes, it was a media event, and getting good video was easy. However, one thing that happened comes to mind. One of the large officers on Dennerll's team was known as "Big Foot"—a huge man. I came around a corner with a cameraman and saw Big Foot holding a suspected dealer from the back by his belt and his shirt collar. He was using the guy like a belt sander on a brick wall. He gave us a look and we turned away and went back around the corner. It was a kind of professional courtesy back then. Now, with the help of 20/20 vision and a rear-view mirror, it is clear that we made the wrong choice. The shot should have been used. Back then, we didn't even shoot it.

It probably would be a lawsuit today. I am just describing how it was back in the day, not defending it. They did their jobs, we covered it, and when we got into tough spots, they were there to have our backs. The man arrested was convicted for possession of a substantial amount of marijuana and whet (a street term for marijuana laced with PCP or some other hallucinogenic drug).

The Red Truck

Another night, we were to meet Roger and his crew in front of the television station. The crew was there, but Roger was running late. I was talking to Detective Bill Leonard. As we talked, a red truck drove by. It appeared the driver had no shirt on and was staring at Bill and me. After that, he drove a hundred yards or so and talked to two young men walking near the old Pat Joyce Tavern on East 6th Street. After a brief talk, he drove off. Bill, being a seasoned officer, noticed this suspicious behavior. "I'm going across the street in front of the school board to see if he comes back," he said. Bill was sitting on a stone wall about two feet high and the man came back. Bill later said that he was "making eyes at me."

Enter Roger. He was late and wanted to get busy. He asked me, "Where's Leonard?" I pointed to him and he yelled across the street to Bill to come over to us. Bill protested, saying that he needed another minute or two. Roger wouldn't hear of it, "Come on we're late, let's get going." Bill obeyed.

Cameraman Dave Hollis and I got into the back of the police car and we took off. As we turned onto one of the streets on the other side of the school board, I saw the red truck. I told Roger that it was the truck Bill had been talking about. He radioed Bill, who was in another car, and Bill explained what had been going on. Roger decided to pull the red truck over.

When the truck pulled over, Roger and Detective Pam Nicholson got out of the front seat of the police car and walked toward the truck. The driver appeared to be reaching for something beneath his seat. The officers pulled their guns out and Roger yelled, "Get out of the car." The man was still reaching under the seat. "Show your hands," Roger said. "That's a good way to get shot." Roger went to the car, reached through the driver's window, and began to pull the man out. The door popped open and out came the driver. He was fully nude except for his pants around his ankles. That was something I didn't expect!

Roger had him put his hands up on a wall and began to question him. "Sir, what is going on with you?" The driver, still naked, said nothing was going on. "Sir, you are driving around the streets of our city with no clothes on propositioning every male you see," Roger said. "I think there *is* something going on with you." The man asked if he could pull up his pants, which were still around his ankles. "Yeah, pull 'em up," Roger barked. Turns out he had been reaching for his pants when he didn't immediately show his hands.

Several weeks later my wife, Kim, and I went out to dinner. A waiter approached our table. It was the man from the arrest. He turned on his heel and walked out of the restaurant. Never saw him again!

West 80th Street Drug Bust

We had a real stroke of luck one night on Lorain Avenue. Roger and his crew went busting into a second-floor apartment on West 80th Street. We were right behind them with our camera rolling. We got in so quickly that no one noticed. They arrested the man living there and found a big stash of drugs. Roger or one of his crew got the idea to not take the guy to jail right away. They cuffed him to a radiator and decided to wait for his customers to show up. They did. There were several more arrests when people looking for drugs came to the door. One in particular stands out.

A woman knocked and said enough to one of the undercover guys to indicate that she was looking for drugs. She was arrested. She denied being there to buy dope. She was patted down, and they found a crack pipe in her pants pocket. One of the detectives said, "if you're not here to buy drugs, what is this for?" Her reply was classic. "These are not my pants; these are my cousin's pants." You can't make this stuff up.

Stage Door and New Era Burlesque

You probably get the idea that Roger liked the community to know what he was doing. Getting on TV made that happen. A quick example of this was when his unit busted two notorious strip joints on Prospect Avenue near where Cleveland State's Wolstein Center is today. Stage Door Johnny's and The New Era Burlesque were the names. Both had booths with privacy curtains. A dancer would do private dances—and more, once the curtain closed. The payment came in the form of the dancer charging the customer for a bottle of Champagne. Two or three hundred dollars was average.

The bust went down quickly, and Roger had an order to padlock the place. But he didn't do it immediately. He waited till 6 p.m. the next day. His reasoning was simple: that way, the TV stations would carry it live. He was right. At the stroke of 6, there he was, live on-air with an electric drill putting a padlock on the place.

I Wasn't the Only One

Marty Savidge, a great reporter, has worked for CNN and NBC. Here in Cleveland he worked at WJW, Channel 8. One night I was headed over to the Sixth District police headquarters, where I had planned to meet Roger and his crew. When I walked into the lobby, there was Marty. He got a funny look on his face, almost a concerned look. I didn't know he'd be there, and clearly he didn't know I would be. Or so I thought. Marty had one of the first cell phones in town—it was about as big as a brick and had a long antenna sticking out of it. I was puzzled when, after seeing me, he quickly left to make a call without saying anything to me. Unusual for Marty, a friendly guy whom I knew well. Something must be up, I thought.

I saw that he left his notes on his chair when he went out to make the call. I needed to figure out what was going on. I went over and had a glance at the notes. It seemed that the prominent and popular Cleveland State basketball coach had been arrested on drug charges. I was screwed.

I used a pay phone to call the TV station and we threw everything we had at the story, but we couldn't catch up; Marty's cameraman already had video of the arrest. Kudos to him. I never told him this story. Marty, if you're reading this, I'm sorry about the snooping but all is fair in love and ratings war. Anyway, you beat me badly.

OFFICER JIM SIMONE

I don't know how many lives Jim Simone has, but he risked as many as he had while protecting Cleveland and his beloved Second District. He and I got off to a rocky start because I was young and dumb. Someone called me with some negative information on Simone. Stupidly, I thought, *This is a great story* and started looking into it. After that, the few times I saw Simone, he gave me a look each time. It was clear that he knew I was asking questions about him.

Over time I found no truth to the negative information I'd been given. Clearly someone he had arrested had a beef with him and was trying to dirty him up. As I said, I was young and maybe a little gullible. Duh!

One morning, I saw Simone at municipal court. I walked over and said, "Officer Simone, I'm Paul Orlousky. I guess you know I've been looking into some stuff about you. There is nothing there." He gave me what I came to know as a Simone smirk, as if to say, *No shit.* Then he smiled and said, "You know, you're not like the rest of the weasels that do your job." We became friends.

His Camera Was His Partner

Simone was given a video camera by Mothers Against Drunk Drivers many years ago. He taped every one of his shifts and has volumes of them categorized at his home. He also kept a copy of every police report he ever wrote. There is no challenging him in court. He has arrested a police chief's son, his superior officer, a city council member, and many others. In Jim's view, the law is the law, and it should be applied equally to everyone.

He has had his share of controversies. Jim is afraid of nothing. He was wounded twice in Vietnam. Once almost mortally. He told me that as he was going into surgery the doctor told him, "When you wake up, you'll be in heaven." Imagine hearing those words. I can't. Is there any wonder he is a tough guy?

The Shootings

Jim was a part of five police shootings in which people were killed. He has also been commended by the city for de-escalating situations in which a person's intent was clearly "suicide by police."

I have a story to tell about his last fatal shooting. Jim walked into a bank just as a guy tried to rob the place. Jim tried to apprehend him, but the shooter fled in a pickup truck. When he drove onto a dead-end street, he was trapped. He got out and pointed a gun at Jim. Jim shot him and killed him.

Later that day, I called Jim at home. "Hey Jim, it's Paul Orlousky, I'm not calling for work. You OK?" He said, "Yeah, shook up like always. It's just what comes next. I'll be off the street. The *Plain Dealer* will be all over me. You know." I tried to encourage him, saying that it would be OK. "Paul, have you ever walked into a live bank robbery?" he asked me. I said no. "Do you know anyone who has ever walked into a live bank robbery?" he asked. I said no again. "I've walked into three," he said. "I'm a policeman. I'm supposed to stop it." Wow!

I tried to make him smile. "Jim, you'd better get direct deposit and stay out of banks." He said, "I only went there to get dimes for my grandkids. I have piggy banks for each of them at my house. Every time they come, I put one in their bank." His bravado was no bull, but behind it was a loving, devoted family man.

A Philosophy

Jim says 15% of the officers on the force make 85% of the arrests. The Cleveland Police Department will probably have statistics to say otherwise, but I still believe Jim. He told me that one time on the job he heard on the police radio a report of an active shooting. He immediately headed to the scene. On the way there, he saw two police cars driving away from the situation. He got involved. After the situation was taken care of, the cars he had seen driving away showed up. They transported the prisoners and listed themselves as the arresting officers on two felony cases. At the time he told me the story, he had retired from the Cleveland Police Department. He told it with a shrug, as if to say, *That's how it is these days.*

When Jim was a rookie he walked a beat in the area around East 105th Street and Superior Avenue. He had a nightstick, a gun, a flashlight, and no radio. He would go from call box to call box to let dispatch know where he was or if he needed help. He told me that in those days he'd see some guys blocking a sidewalk where an elderly person was trying to get past. He would tell them, "Move your ass outta the way." If they didn't, he said, he would give them a swift kick in the ass and they would move.

The point to his story was not brutality; he told me that if he had that same interaction today, a guy he might have kicked back then would instead likely have to be arrested and appear in court, and would possibly get a criminal record. "All of that when all he needed was a kick in the ass. These days, the system can create criminals."

After retiring from Cleveland, Simone took part-time jobs in suburbs. I asked him how he liked it. He said he missed the "action," but one thing was nice. "When they wave at you out here, they use all five fingers."

No Fear

The Vietnam wounds weren't the only ones Jim suffered. Once I reported a series of stories using Jim's many video tapes. He had been shot in the face, hit by cars, crashed cars, dragged by cars, and had delivered great lines to criminals like, "Put your hands up, or the next person you're gonna meet is your maker." Many years later, when Jim was over sixty, a woman jumped into the ice-filled Cuyahoga River. A lot of officers were standing by trying to figure out a rescue plan. Jim got there, jumped in without hesitation, and pulled her to shore with the help of a rope that had been tossed his way. He became quite ill afterward. But to respond any other way, I believe, is something that never entered his mind.

That Ain't Gonna Happen

I will end my tales about Jim Simone with the last news story we did together. I knew he was going to retire, and I wanted to ride along with him on his last night. The department made me jump over a lot of hurdles to get the OK, but I did. It wasn't like the old days when I could just call a police sergeant and ask, "Can we come along?" They even made me and cameraman Marty DeChant each get a million-dollar liability policy.

I had asked Simone about the two of us riding along with him on that last night. His response was quick. "No way. All you want to do is get me crying, and that ain't gonna happen." I said, "OK, how about the night before you retire?" He agreed. We met him at 11 p.m.

We weren't four blocks out of the Second District headquarters when he turned the overhead lights on. A driver clearly had gone through a red light, and Jim ticketed him. The rest of the night was busy—a guy on a bicycle hit by a car at a gas station, a suburban woman turning tricks on Detroit Avenue for crack. She was so emaciated that she slipped out of her handcuffs twice on the way to the lockup, only to be cuffed again. He also made his last DUI arrest. There had been thousands of others over the years.

Then came a call about someone breaking into a home. We sped there. Arriving at the home, we saw another police car coming from the opposite direction. Jim was wearing a microphone for the evening. I couldn't hear it, but Marty could. The cops ran around the building chasing the suspect, with us following. The guy was clearly high as a kite. They asked him why he was there. "It's my friend's house," he answered. Why was he going through a window? "My friend didn't answer the door." "What was his friend's name?" "Uh, it's kind of a long name." The officers led him to the car saying, "Let's go." As they sat him in the car, he stopped and said, "Officers, I just want to thank you for not whoopin' my ass." I laughed. "We gotta use that," I said to Marty. He replied, "It's better than that—I'll show you back at the station."

We had coffee with Jim toward the end of the shift, and left before he filled out the many reports he'd have to write about his busy night. Back at the TV station, Marty put the tape in the player and showed me what he had mentioned earlier. Remember, Jim was wearing a microphone, and as the officers from the other car met him running to the back yard, he said, "I got TV with me." He likely was telling them to watch their language. However, it is also possible that what that suspect said about avoiding an ass whoopin was also thanks to a TV camera being there.

CHIEF ED KOVACIC

Police Chief Edward Kovacic once called Jim Simone "the best cop I have ever known." That is high tribute, coming from Kovacic. If you have ever seen the movie *Kill the Irishman*, he is the detective played by Val Kilmer. He investigated mob activity in Cleveland, including the exploits of Irish mobster Danny Greene. Eventually he investigated Danny Greene's killing by a car bomb. The Italian mob had planted it. During his investigation mobsters turned state's evidence, which led to the conviction of many, including the Mafia Don of Cleveland, James "Jack White" Licavoli. It led to the downfall of the mob in Cleveland.

I always wondered why they didn't use Kovacic's name in the movie, so I asked him. He told me that he refused to let them use it if the movie ever showed him in a bar with the mob. It did. Up to that point he had provided the filmmakers with background, but he couldn't agree to the portrayal, and the Kilmer character's name was changed. He was that kind of standup guy. I can't imagine anyone in Cleveland would ever have the balls to offer Ed Kovacic a bribe or to try to fix a case. He'd probably use one of his favorite terms if someone tried: "I'd have to put the boots to him." You get the drift.

Put in a different way, there is only one picture of any Cleveland police chief at the Cleveland Police Patrolmen's Association hall, the union's headquarters. It is Ed Kovacic. The relationship between a chief and the troops can be contentious. The troops respected Kovacic because he was one of them. He came up through the ranks and earned the respect. But as boss he was no pushover. He expected much from his officers and got it. When they screwed up, he came down hard.

"The Chief," as he is fondly remembered, had an expectation of the media as well. I had done a story about some officers messing something up. He disciplined them. I was about to find out what his discipline felt like.

Late one day all the TV stations were notified of a 5 p.m. briefing at the Chief's conference room on the ninth floor of police headquarters. We had no clue what it was about. All the TV stations and the newspapers got there, and in came Chief Kovacic. He launched into a ten-minute tirade—about me! In particular, how my recent news story "Cream Puff Cops," about cops goofing off, had been unfair. I tried to counter. "But Chief, just this afternoon you disciplined these officers for exactly what I reported," I protested. Made no difference; he wouldn't listen to it. Clearly no other station was going to report on this news conference. The chief was making his point by dressing me down in front of my peers. I still believe my news story was a fair one. But Ed was making another point: that he was always there for his troops. That briefing went miles in telling them he had their backs.

The Chief and I had always had a great relationship. About a week later I saw him at an event, and it was like nothing had happened. I was kind of sheepish at first and he said, "Hey Paul, how's it going?" It was like the father that scolded his child about something and moved on to the next page.

I consulted the Chief on many topics over the years, even well after he'd retired. Marty and I would go to his house and talk to him on video about the story I was doing. That took three or four minutes. Then after we stopped rolling, we would tell stories about our exploits for two hours. He was that engaging.

Chief Kovacic died in 2018. I attended his wake. It was at the Cathedral of Saint John the Evangelist, and the line was long. I went up to the casket and there he was, looking proud as always, in his chief's uniform. Next, I saw his beloved wife Barbara. She had always been there during our long talks at the house. By this point she was blind. One of their daughters said "Mom, this is Paul Orlousky." She smiled, grabbed my hand warmly and said, "You know Paul, you were always Ed's favorite." I am welling up as I write this. I hope anyone who knew that man at some level would be able to hear that kind of tribute about their work. I will never forget it. Barbara, his partner forever, died just a few weeks later. That likely tells you all you need to know about the bond the two had. Her support and love for him, and his support and love for her. I am blessed having known them.

DET. MARVIN CROSS

Marv Cross is one of the most likable people you'll ever meet. He came from the streets and knew the streets well. He worked at various times with Sgt. Dennerll's vice unit and a variety of other assignments.

One encounter I had with Marv shows why I liked being out on the streets reporting instead of being in the studio sitting at the anchor desk—and why you can't prepare for every situation. This incident happened in the 1990s. Looking back at it years later with the benefit of 20/20 hindsight, you might question what I did at the time and why. But this is what happened.

A cameraman and I were returning downtown on the Shoreway

from the East Side. I heard a call on the police scanner and recognized Marv's voice. He and his partner were chasing someone. The next call gave a location, Gordon Park. We were about to drive right past, so we turned in to check it out.

As we drove up, I saw Marv cuffing a guy on the ground. We got out of the car and ran toward him.

"Paul," Marv said, "sit on this guy right here. We gotta go get the other guy."

I obliged, and Marv ran off in the direction his partner had gone.

This turned out to be awkward on two levels.

On one level, after a minute or so sitting on the suspect, it became extremely uncomfortable. For me, that is; I'm sure it was for him, too. Thankfully, he wasn't trying to get up. His hands were behind his back and he was face down on the ground.

"How's it goin'?" I asked.

All he said was "F*** you, a**hole."

I figured I'd better not say anything more. Just a couple of minutes later, Marv and his partner came back with the second suspect.

On another level, there is an ethical question: Was it proper for me as a journalist to assist in an arrest? At the time, I didn't think twice about it; I was helping catch someone accused of a serious crime. I had that rush of adrenaline that I always craved, and never thought twice about it. Today, though, such an action might be judged differently.

Over the years Marv would sometimes call me with a story idea or a tip. You could take his word to the bank. He rose through the ranks of the Cleveland Police Department, eventually retiring as acting deputy chief. After that he went to work for the Cleveland Cavaliers, working directly on security for the team's new number one draft pick, LeBron James. It was a great hire. LeBron got good advice from the start.

ORLO WANTS TO KNOW

THE CITY OF CLEVELAND INVESTIGATIONS

The City of Cleveland under Mayor Frank Jackson tends to react to problems rather than being proactive. This led to a treasure trove of stories for me. We turned it into a segment, "Orlo Wants to Know." I would get a tip from a citizen who had been unable to get action from the city, or I would notice a problem myself. We'd go out and shoot it and ask the city for a reaction. I'd get none, then do the story and point out the problem. In pretty short order, the problem would get fixed. The city never got in front of their problems. I often would tell their spokesman, "Call when you get it fixed and I'll report that you fixed it." He never did.

I have lots of specifics. Some are laughable, others sad. Overgrown trees so dense that streetlights didn't illuminate the street. Cemetery plots flooded with water; headstones toppled over for years by tree roots. Once, the city removed a crosswalk at a blind man's home. He had to cross a busy street to get to the supermarket, and was in danger of being hit every day. He called and called and got no answer from the city. I reported it on TV, and two weeks later the crosswalk signs were back—along with one of those boxes that beep to let you know when it's safe to cross. Wouldn't it have been better to just respond to the citizen in the first place? At least say you're going to handle it. Instead, the city got dragged through the mud repeatedly.

Silly Stuff

Sometimes, minor problems that could easily have been fixed but weren't became excellent visuals for TV. Picture these: An abandoned home—the next-door neighbor took photos of a raccoon looking out the window at him for weeks, but the city wouldn't help. A family received a $12,000 water bill for a single month's usage—enough water to more than fill an Olympic-sized swimming pool (they didn't own one)—and the Cleveland Water Department wouldn't relent. Grass left to grow so tall on baseball fields that when kids knelt down they couldn't be seen; the city did nothing until a player got hurt. One of my favorites was a homeowner who sent me a photo of his garbage bin stuck in a tree in front of his home. The arm on the city's garbage truck must have malfunctioned, and the crew just left the bin in the tree.

Serious Stuff

Lack of information from the city became serious in 2019, when computer systems at Cleveland Hopkins Airport were hacked. For more than a week there was no ground communication, and flight display boards in the terminal were blank. We kept asking the city what the problem was. Eventually, we started asking if it was a hack. The city denied it. Reporters asked outside experts, who almost to a person said it had to be a hack. The city denied it again and again.

Finally, they held a press conference at which they admitted that the computers had been hacked. Everyone was livid. Information that the public had every right to know had been purposely withheld. We had valid questions: What was the city doing about it? Could it happen again? Why were their security systems so lax?

When they opened the floor to questions, I was the first to ask. "You just admitted what every reporter in town has known for a week—you were hacked. Why didn't you admit it?" Silence from the podium. I leaned over to the spokesman, who had denied it repeatedly, and asked him by name. Silence. Finally, the mayor's chief of staff gave an answer that I thought was b.s. The rest of the briefing was vicious. All the veteran reporters smelled blood and jumped in. The city not only came out with egg on its face, but its face had been bloodied. The administration's credibility, which was already low with me, had just disappeared. Why? Because they didn't get out in front of anything. Denial of a problem is not good government.

Deadly Stuff

Here's an example of how Mayor Jackson was loyal to a fault. Cuyahoga County Common Pleas Court Judge Lance Mason had gotten in serious trouble. He was arrested for beating his wife Aisha while driving in a car as their two children were riding in the back seat. He broke bones in her face by repeatedly punching her and slamming her face into the dashboard. Police arrested him, and he was convicted and sent to prison.

When Mason got out of prison, Mayor Jackson hired him for a job in his administration. No one was told. I went to a briefing on a different topic at City Hall, saw Mason there, and wondered why. I asked, and he told me that he was working for the mayor. I was surprised. "Good luck," I said. Not in a sarcastic way; I meant it. He had always been good to me when I had covered cases in his courtroom. I thought he was a fair judge, a soft-spoken guy, and I never would have thought was able to do what he had been sent to prison for.

Later, the Jackson administration was asked about Mason being hired. The administration spokesman repeatedly dodged the question. That caused such a stir that the mayor eventually was forced to come out and talk about it. There were many good questions. How was Mason picked for the job? What did he do? Were others considered? The mayor said that he was a firm believer in second chances, and that Mason was doing a good job.

Several months later, Mason was arrested for murdering his now-ex-wife Aisha in front of their two children as he appeared for a pre-arranged visitation. So much for second chances. Lance

Mason got a second chance; Aisha Mason didn't. Mason was convicted of murder and received a life sentence.

TROUBLE AT THE KENNEL

For contrast, here's a story about how another Cleveland mayor's administration dealt with incompetence by getting in front of it and making changes.

In the 1980s and 1990s, the Cleveland Kennel was a hell hole. It smelled horribly. Cages were piled in concrete rows, one on top of another. There was a channel at the back of each where waste should be hosed, and then flushed away. One problem: The animals weren't being taken out of the cages for the cleaning and disinfecting process.

A volunteer at the kennel tipped me off, but it was going to be difficult for us to prove. I had to get video. Luckily, the tipster was crafty. We made a small box that concealed a camera. There was a shelf that was close to an electrical outlet. The tipster took the box in one day and plugged it in. We had a timer attached so that it would go on a couple of minutes before the day began for the workers.

It performed like a charm. What we taped was horrendous. Rather than remove the dogs from the cages, workers just went down the rows with a strong hose. Not a fire hose, but not your garden hose either. Through the bars of the cages they sprayed, the dogs cowering to avoid the harsh spray. Next, they went down the rows with a pump sprayer of disinfectant and again just sprayed it through the front of the cages. It soaked the dogs and anything else in the way.

The kill room was not in our view, but we watched as dog after dog was dragged in that direction. Many had their paws in front of them trying to stop while they were being led. None ever came out of the room. Maybe they sensed what was coming?

We confronted the boss of the kennel and eventually, we asked Mayor Mike White what he was going to do about it. He had a strong response. Even before our story aired, he fired the boss, and workers were either fired or reassigned. A new boss and protocols were installed. When our story aired, it generated a massive outpouring of anger.

The new boss, John Baird, changed the culture there for a decade. He joked with me for years that he owed his job to me. In 2019, thanks to his efforts, a new and updated Cleveland Kennel was opened, with far more humane conditions, state-of-the-art ventilation, and other updates. I have no doubt that it will lead to many more adoptions.

SPEED CAMERAS IN EAST CLEVELAND

Other municipalities are just as guilty as Cleveland of ignoring citizen complaints. After all, it works! Eventually those complaining citizens, and sometimes even reporters, just get tired and go away. East Cleveland is chief among them.

East Cleveland has controversial speed cameras. I reported stories on speed cameras in other towns, like Linndale and Newburgh Heights. Mayors always claim they are being used for safety, not revenue. In my view, they are full of crap. East Cleveland may be the worst of all. They have a speed camera in a school zone for a school that is permanently closed. It is illegal, but what working person can take the time to go to court to fight it? They either pay the ticket or don't pay and move on with their lives.

The law says there must be a sign warning that a speed enforcement area is ahead. East Cleveland didn't have one for a particularly notorious revenue-generating camera. A viewer complained to us about it. We did a story, and the ticket was dropped. Some cities will continue their problematic activities until they get caught by someone like a TV reporter who can show what's going on to a wider audience. One citizen asking for justice is ignored. The warning sign never went up, and the city continued to collect illegal fines.

A CONSTIPATED COURT

For months, a nurse living in public housing in East Cleveland had been trying to buy a home. She had saved a down payment, but her mortgage was denied. She discovered that she had some outstanding tickets on East Cleveland's court docket. She had paid them and had the proof, but the Clerk of Courts hadn't processed her payments, and as a result she had a blemish on her credit. She asked about it repeatedly but got no answers. So she came to us, I got in touch with Judge William Dawson in East Cleveland Municipal Court, and quickly he got it fixed. Months later, the caller showed us the home she was able to buy, and I also saw a broad smile that we were able to help put on her face with a couple of simple phone calls. Her own phone calls to the city should have had the same clout as mine, but they didn't.

BLIND TO A BLINDING SNOW

Imagine driving under a highway overpass and suddenly having a blinding sheet of ice and snow dumped onto your car from a city snow plow driving past, high above. That happened to a driver in Warrensville Heights. His view of the road was blinded, but he was able to recover and maintained control of his vehicle. His new truck, though, now had a dented hood from the weight of the ice and snow. He complained to the city several times, but nothing was done. The city even denied it was their truck that had plowed the snow—despite the fact that the citizen provided an accurate description of it. The city used red trucks that no one else in the area used.

Next, he complained to me. I contacted the city and got a service boss to admit it was their truck. Next, I had to confront the mayor about the discrepancy. He told me he'd investigate it. Nothing happened. After that came a couple of follow-ups with the city law director, who repeatedly denied the claim. We reported on the city's repeated claim to the truck owner that it was being handled.

Our persistent pestering worked. In the end, after our continued prodding, the guy got his damage paid for. Does it really have to come to this?

Stories like this kept me employed, and I enjoyed helping folks, but after a while they tend to erode your faith in local government. It shouldn't take a TV camera in their faces to make city administrators do the right thing.

STORIES THAT STUCK WITH ME

YOU SEE A LOT AS a reporter, and not all of it is pleasant. My first odd story was within a few months of getting a job in Cleveland. There was a shooting just off Chester Avenue around East 70th Street or so. A young boy had found a pistol in the apartment where he lived with several siblings. Playing with the gun, he fired and killed one of his brothers. We were at the scene when the coroner brought the body out. As it came down the steps of a dilapidated row house, one of the other siblings jumped in front of the camera and began waving and making noise. It hit me. His dead brother was being carried away, but being on television was more important to him. *Should television be that important?* I thought.

The next was when Pete Miller and I were sent to do a story about a fatal accident at an intersection on Route 303 in Brunswick. We got there, found someone who had either heard or seen the crash, and shot video of various car parts left at the scene. As we were leaving, I leaned down and found a penny in the street. I picked it up. "Hey Pete, a lucky penny," I said. "Orlo, I don't think that is a lucky one," Pete replied. It hit me that it probably came from the victim's pocket or car. I quickly threw it back down. I was spooked!

Another was the suicide in 1985 of Dr. Frederick Holliday, a gentle and kind man who honestly believed he could make a change in the Cleveland school system. He was sadly mistaken. He was pushing computer education long before it was in vogue. Problem was that he was plagued, in my estimation, by a broken system. A million dollars' worth of computers (a huge amount at that time) were purchased and delivered—and they never saw the light of day. Somehow, they disappeared! How does that happen?

In my view, Holliday was also hamstrung by a school board comprised of politically connected people who put personal agendas ahead of the needs of the children of Cleveland. Holliday summed up his frustration by committing suicide in one of the district's high schools. He left a note, and we were given a copy by the police department. I have kept it all these decades.

He had been in Cleveland only two years but couldn't take any more. In his note, which he titled "An Open Letter to the People of Cleveland," he wrote, "The events of the past few weeks makes my reporting to work meaningless. The purpose seems to be lost. There is a mindlessness that has nothing to do with the education of children or the welfare of the city. This hurts most of all." At the end he said, "Use this event to rid yourselves of petty politics, racial politics, greed, hate and corruption. This city deserves better. The children deserve better. Cleveland deserves better. I have no malice for anyone. Only love and sadness." I'm not sure anyone listened!

A HOME RUN

No ball had ever been hit into the center-field bleachers at the old Cleveland Municipal Stadium during a major-league ballgame. Mickey Mantle hit one far enough, but it landed in a walkway between the bleachers and the left-field stands. In 1983, the night before the opening day game, I did the usual TV story with a visit to the locker room, showing the uniforms all neatly pressed and everything else that you might expect. I had to do a live shot at 11 p.m. How could I make this different?

I asked longtime Indians clubhouse man Cy Buynak for a ball and a bat, which he lent to me. I did my live intro to the story, and then when they came back to me live, I announced that no one had ever hit a ball into the center-field bleachers, but I was about to do it. I let the viewers know that the camera was in the bleachers. I tossed the ball into the air, hit it, and it whizzed uncomfortably close to the camera. How did I do it? The camera pulled out and showed that I was in center field and had only hit the ball about 100 feet or so. A memorable end to a routine story. I still have the ball; it has a blue scuff mark from where it hit a bench in the bleachers.

MY FIRST "GOTCHA" MOMENT

A woman complained to me that she had gone to a job interview and the owner of the company had suggested that being a "playmate for him would be a plus in getting hired." She was outraged. I thought that this would be hard to prove. However, she said she wasn't alone. Other women she knew claimed to have had similar experiences. I asked her to have them contact me. One woman came forward, then a second, and a third. *OK, this may need an undercover person,* I thought.

I had a good relationship with Cleveland Women Working, a group that advocated for equal rights, pay, and treatment of all workers in hiring and employment. They provided me with a feisty advocate who would likely be hit on by the owner. She sent in her résumé and he set up an interview. She went in with us rolling from the surveillance van. The owner was coy at first, but certainly sexually suggestive. Our undercover applicant never gave any indication of anything more than an interest in the job that was advertised.

After a few days, he called her back for a second interview. Cameraman Bob Wilkinson and I drove to the business ahead of her and were in the van, getting video, when she arrived. She went in, wearing a wireless microphone. The owner was subtle at first. As she continued to rebuff his suggestions, they became more obvious. Finally, he said it: "Look, I am looking for someone to bend over the desk for me a couple of times a week in order to get this job."

I'm sure she wanted to punch him, but I am thankful she didn't.

If she had, it would have blown up the whole investigation. After the interview ended, I tried to confront the owner on camera, but he got in his Mercedes and drove off.

As is so often the case, the phone began to ring the next day at the TV station. The first call was to the general manager, who told me the guy said he was an acquaintance of his and bought advertising time on the station. The GM ignored the call and asked me about my story. I told him what I had, and he said to go with it.

The more important part of the story is that other women who had worked for this man called me. They confirmed all that we had on tape. One said that he had demanded that she work on New Year's Day, and when she arrived at work he called her to the coffee room. There he was, with a $100 bill wrapped around himself. I will leave that to your imagination, but it won't take you too long to figure it out.

I learned later that when the business owner found out the date our story was to air on TV, he surprised his wife with a Caribbean vacation (in those days there was only a small likelihood that anyone would have taped the newscast, and the internet was nonexistent), and he dodged a bullet!

WHAT'S IN THE BOX?

This was a great tip. If I had had a less supportive general manager, it might never have seen the air. A company was selling circuit boards to the United States Army. These were backup boards for artillery batteries that were being used in the Persian Gulf. The specifications said that the boards were to be packaged a certain way, put into boxes a certain way, and then sealed so that no moisture or dust could get inside. They were shipped to a huge government storage facility in central Pennsylvania.

The specifications also said that the boxes would never be opened. My tipster worked in the shipping area of the company. He saw that what was being put into the boxes were just junk circuit boards. The owner had seen the opportunity for fraud in the specification that said the boxes wouldn't be opened. The tipster, a shipping clerk, clearly had a beef with the owner.

When we visited, the confrontation with the owner was classic. He was very accommodating. He obviously figured he could pull the wool over our eyes as he had done with the government. A real b.s. artist. His defense was that the boards weren't expensive items. "If you're gonna cheat, you're gonna cheat with something expensive, not those," he told me. It seemed to show that he had some experience about how and where to cheat. Not a smart statement to make in front of a TV camera!

A federal investigation followed, and eventually an underling took the fall for the crime. Many years later, I was in federal court for a hearing on another matter. A man walking out of the previous hearing gave me a strange look. It was the owner of the computer company. "Don't worry," I said. "I'm not here for you." He quickly walked away. I found out later that he had been indicted for pulling the same ruse with a new company. This time he was promising hospitals to pay for old, outdated equipment. He'd buy it, never pay for it, and then resell it to other hospitals without delivering it. This time he went to prison.

Management had my back big time on my initial story about the computer parts. My boss, a high-ranking executive at the station, had a daughter who worked at the computer company. He got a call from the company's owner, who was trying to kill the story. I was called upstairs to my boss's office. It was awkward, and I didn't know what to expect. "I suspect you know why I called you," he said. I told him I did. "Are you sure of the facts?" he asked. No; I said that I was 100% certain. "OK, go with it," he said. After the story aired, my boss's daughter was fired. But once again justice prevailed. She won a large settlement for wrongful termination.

GENIUS OF THE WEEK

Our sweeps series "Genius of the Week" was a direct rip-off of a series of beer commercials appearing at the time. Each began with me doing a fake baritone voice saying, "Here's to you (fill in the name here)…" just like the beer commercials. Then engineer Mike Suchecki (who sang in a rock band and had a great voice) would imitate the short musical interludes from the commercials. Each week we highlighted a story that was worth mentioning, but not worth a full investigation.

The first story was about the Ohio Legislature and its debate over legislation involving exotic dancers. They argued about a law that limited how close a customer could come to a stripper. This was happening when the recession was in its early stages—clearly at a time when there were many more important topics for lawmakers to be debating.

Another story featured an off-duty police officer who stopped traffic for minutes at a time to allow people in the parking garage he worked for to get its patrons into traffic first. It tied up a busy street for blocks. Mike sang, "What the [bleep] is going on?" (bleeped by a car horn) over video of a driver throwing his hands into the air.

One was when transit police were granted the authority to write traffic and parking tickets. They went nuts, writing far more than the Cleveland Police Department. Our singer said, "My pen's runnin' out of ink." Then it was the County Commissioners' crazy purchase of a long-abandoned skyscraper for potential use as a new county administration building. They spent millions on asbestos abatement and other improvements before selling it to a private developer—at a huge loss to county taxpayers.

The news director didn't like these stories. "I don't get them," he said. I asked the assistant news director, "Why does he not get them? They are about as subtle as a fart in an elevator." He just shrugged. I told cameraman Marty DeChant, and he was enraged. "We're gonna enter them in the Emmy Awards next year." I agreed, figuring he'd forget. Eleven months later, Marty came to me asking for my portion of the Emmy Award entry fee. I said we should forget about it. He insisted, so we entered. We won that year for best feature!

AUTO EMISSIONS TESTING

An elderly gentleman called me and said that his car had failed the state-mandated E-Check vehicle emissions test. However, he claimed that he was told by the inspector that if he came back with cash, his car would pass. The caller, a World War II veteran who had served his country and worked hard all his life, was not happy about the shakedown effort.

I asked him if he would go back and retake the test. He agreed. He was street smart and was able to get his car in the line with the same inspector. We would shoot video from the parking lot and get audio from a microphone the man was wearing. When his turn came, he offered her the cash. She rebuffed him and told him that she couldn't take it inside the facility. She told him to leave and meet her in the parking lot. There, she scolded him again for trying to give her the money inside the testing station. Then he gave her the money and drove back through the line for the emissions test. His car went through again and passed. We shot the entire exchange.

After the man left, we confronted her on camera and she denied everything. We had it all on tape, including her taking the money and scolding him for offering it inside the station where the transaction might have been seen or recorded by internal security.

As is typical when dealing with government agencies, after the story aired, nothing was done about it. They blew this old hero off as some sort of diminished individual because of his age. They ignored the video!

A year or two later I was talking about this story at a social function. The man who headed up the emissions test agency in the Cleveland area was at the same event and overheard the end of the conversation. At some point I went to the restroom. As I stood at a urinal, the same man came up to another urinal. He said, "Yeah, that story was a complete fake. I had a lot of explaining to do after it was on the air." I asked, "How did you explain it? I don't think you remember—I was the reporter who did the story." The smile drained from his face. "Should I put the video on the air again to refresh everyone's memory?" I asked. I have never heard a zipper go up so fast, and the man quickly left the restroom.

FINDING A HORSE FOR A LITTLE GIRL

I had done a story about an animal rescue group going to a farm to rescue several horses that had been neglected. The horses were thin, had burdocks caught in their manes, and hadn't had any hoof care in a long time. My story generated a lot of response. That happened any time I reported a story about animals. There were many offers of financial support, but one call caught my attention. A woman caller said she wanted something—a horse! One specific horse. Her young daughter had seen it on the news and had fallen in love. She explained that her daughter had had a horse, but it had died in a barn fire.

I checked with the animal rescue people. The horse would need time for rehabilitation, but they were interested in the adoption. I put the two sides in contact with one another. Sometime later, I got a call: The horse was ready to be delivered to the little girl. I went with a cameraman to the girl's home for the meeting. It was a magical moment. The little girl immediately took to the horse. I don't speak horse, but it seemed mutual. The girl immediately began brushing and caring for the horse. The rescue group had done the right thing and had made the correct placement.

It was a nice ending to a story, and as a reporter I felt good to have put these people together with a simple minute-and-a-half story on television. It got better. About twenty-five years later, I was in a store when a woman stopped me and said, "You're Paul Orlousky." I agreed that I was. She thanked me again for the story about the horse—and her now-grown daughter. "You will never remember this...," she started. But she was wrong. I clearly remembered the look on that little girl's face. The mother went on to tell me that before our story about the neglected horses, her daughter had been having a hard time because of the loss of her horse in the fire. The quick replacement had made a huge difference in her daughter rebounding from that sad loss and had gotten her back into her life's routine.

She thanked me, and I said, "I was happy to do it, no big deal." I think I probably should have said, "No, thank *you*!"

HORSES TO HORSEMEAT

The next horse story didn't end as well. A couple called me about two of their horses. They were missing. It seems the owner of the stable where the horses were kept had sold the horses for what she claimed was overdue rent for their stalls.

I went to the couple's home, and they showed me paperwork that appeared to prove that the sale was illegal. As it turns out, one of the horses, a thoroughbred named Fighting Flamingo, was sold to a meat packing company that processed horsemeat for use in France. The couple had video of Fighting Flamingo winning a race at Thistledown race track. Great visuals always make great stories.

Cameraman Kevin Dorenkott and I got their side of the story and went to the stable to get the other side. When we got there, the owner was in a large barn, working out a horse. I asked if we could speak to her about the two horses. "Wait right here a minute," she said, and she walked into her home. She was polite, so we waited. The next thing we heard was a siren. Yes, it was police coming for us.

A young officer got out of the police car and started yelling at us to get off the property, telling us that we were trespassing. He was not a bit polite. I tried to tell him that she had told us to wait right where we were standing. He wouldn't hear of it. Luckily for us, a supervisor soon arrived, an older and more experienced officer. He was calm and asked what was going on. I explained, including the harsh treatment by the younger officer. He said, "She told you to leave." I said she hadn't. He said, "Well she does want you to leave, and my officer told you to leave as well." I told him that she had not, and that I was trying to explain that to the first officer just as the supervisor arrived.

This is where keeping the camera rolling paid off. "They're telling you an interesting story, Lieutenant," I said, "because we have been rolling on this entire incident, and I can prove that you are the first one telling us to leave. I have it on video. And I bet the chief might also want to see the way your officer treated us. Why don't we go over to the car and look at it?" He declined, and said, kind of sheepishly, "She wants you to leave." We left.

Once again a person reacting aggressively—calling the police on us—rather than offering a reasoned explanation made it a better story than it really was!

As it turns out, the owner of the stable was well connected with the police. She provided horses for parades and things like that. It also turns out that after a lawsuit and trial in Cuyahoga County Common Pleas Court, the jury sided with Fighting Flamingo's owners and awarded them $8,500. Still later, an appeal by the stable owner reversed the award. Later, in a higher court, the original ruling was upheld and Fighting Flamingo's owners won the fight. By the way, the other horse that was sold for horsemeat was named Breakin' the Law.

VIDEOGRAPHERS—WITHOUT THEM, I'M RADIO

I LEARNED A GREAT DEAL from the many videographers I worked with over the years. Early in my career, when I would arrive in a new market I quickly I realized they knew a heck of a lot more about that town that I did. So I listened. I never forgot that without them, I would be radio. TV needs pictures.

EDDIE ADAMS

In Binghamton, New York, I learned about more than just the town from WBNG's chief videographer, Eddie Adams. He had been there forever. At my previous station in that city, we had videotape so you could do long interviews. WBNG had high-quality film cameras. These were more expensive and delivered better image quality than the tape I had used previously. But the film had to be developed after it was shot. On my first day at the station, I went out on a story with Eddie. I began to interview someone. I asked one question, then two, then three. After the fourth, I heard the film camera click off. I turned and said, "Is something wrong, Eddie?" He said no, "I'll start rolling when you figure out what you want to ask him. I'm not gonna process all this stuff."

I got a lecture in the car on the way back to the station. The film cost twelve cents a foot, and then it cost ten cents to process each foot. I learned about film, but the lesson was bigger than just film versus videotape. Don't do your background work on camera, I learned. Do your homework before the interview. Then, keep interviews short. It not only saved film, it made the job way easier when I went back to look at the interview later. It takes less time when the video is shorter.

I also learned in Binghamton that any time I had so called "writer's block" while composing a story, it meant I didn't know enough about the story. Make some calls! After that the words just flow.

MIKE WARD

I met Mike Ward at WEWS in Cleveland. He was a videographer at the time. Mike is one of the smartest men I have ever met in my life. There is no subject he was not well versed on. Also, no opinion he would not share with you. He could not tolerate incompetence or complacency. He was passionate in everything I saw him do. I learned much from Mike about marrying words to pictures. I had never realized in the past just how important that marriage is. Mike didn't lecture; he showed us by example. He had little patience for those who didn't get it or couldn't do it.

There is a video clip that you may have seen. It is a Major League Baseball classic. Legendary Baltimore Orioles manager Earl Weaver was angry at the umpires one night at Cleveland Municipal Stadium during a game against the Indians. This was not unusual; Weaver always had a problem with umpires. The game was not televised, but some local stations had cameras there for news coverage. Mike covered it for WEWS. The other photographers probably thought, *Oh, it's only Weaver going off again* and went for a hot dog. Mike sensed something and continued to roll. Weaver stormed back to the dugout, grabbed the rule book, and tore it up in front of the umpires in the middle of the field. If you've ever laughed at that clip, thank Mike Ward.

Mike had a meteoric rise at WEWS to assistant news director, then to Chicago to lead WMAQ, then news director jobs in Philadelphia, Raleigh, and Washington, DC. He had a severe stroke in Washington and couldn't work any longer. Mike died in 2014, but he lives on in Cleveland television because he influenced a generation of reporters and camera people. The way news has been shot and edited in Cleveland since the early 1980s has Mike Ward's stamp on it. Lots of the people I mentioned in this book are disciples of Mike's. Tom Livingston, Rich Geyser, Dave Arnold, Marty DeChant, and too many others to name.

I never would have lasted as long as I did in television if I had never met Mike Ward.

MARTY DECHANT

I wasn't going to write a lot about Marty DeChant in this chapter. No need to, I thought; he is mentioned through this book. That's because he was my partner in crime for about twenty years, almost daily. Marty made me a better reporter. Sometimes, the station would give us a story assignment that we didn't want to do. Marty and I would be prepared, having already shot parts of a story *we* wanted to do, keeping them in our back pockets. Then, when the station assigned an idea we didn't like, I'd usually tell them, "Oh, we gotta do this other story today because I heard another station is on to it. I want to beat them to it." We weren't fooling our assignment editor, Julia Tullos. She was on to us, but she also knew that we delivered every day, so she was our buffer with the dreaded "morning meeting." We were usually out the door by the time the meeting started, and she covered our tracks. As a result of that freedom, I believe we always came up with something worth watching.

Marty was opinionated. We developed a good guy, bad guy relationship. On TV, I appeared the good guy. But it was usually because Marty had paved the way with a blunt question or had refused to turn off the camera when told to do so by someone we were chasing.

Hey Buddy, I Need a Cutaway Shot

One time we were looking for a chiropractor. He had been cited by a state governing body for allowing non-certified technicians to administer X-rays to patients. I was the only one who knew about his sanction. We scoped out his office out but couldn't find him there. But we knew he was also a local politician, and as an elected official was required to attend certain meetings. We went to the next meeting and waited until it ended. I walked up to him. "Doctor, can we talk to you for a minute?" He agreed. I asked about the citation. He was not happy. After a couple of questions, I said thank you and he turned to walk away. Without missing a beat Marty said, "Hey buddy, stay there for minute, I've got to get a cutaway shot." (The term refers to a wider shot showing the two of us.) The guy stayed, staring daggers at me. It was uncomfortable, but Marty got the shot he needed.

Rearranging a Governor's Press Conference

Marty and I went to the Inauguration of Ohio Governor Mike DeWine. We covered the event, and there was to be a question-and-answer session for media afterward in a large room outside his office. Just about every media outlet in the state was there—thirty or more. While we waited, no one said anything about the lighting setup except Marty. He asked the state's audio/video people where the governor was going to be standing. They showed him. "That lighting is all wrong," Marty said. "He's gonna be side-lit. It will look terrible." The A/V people didn't respond, so Marty just walked up and started changing the lighting. He was so confident (and, by the way, correct) that they just stood by and watched. The new governor entered and held the press conference. When it ended, many of the other videographers who had seen the same problem but hadn't had the guts to say anything came up to Marty and thanked him.

Getting There First

Getting to a scene quickly or being the first one to confront somebody in legal trouble is imperative. They'll come to the door the first time someone knocks; after that, any reporters who knock are out of luck. We always joked that when we got a good exclusive or confrontation on a Monday morning it put us in a good mood all week.

You never know how people will react in a situation. Here is one that puzzled us. As usual, Marty and I were out the door early. There had been a lot of wind damage after heavy rains overnight. Tree limbs were down and lots of wires had come down with them. We toured around West Side communities, stopping, getting video of damage, and talking to people. We spotted a power company crew making a repair to wires on the outside of a home. To stay off a busy street, we pulled onto the driveway apron. It was completely innocent. The homeowner came charging out, swearing, asking what we were doing and why we were there, and he told us to go away. You never know how people will react to a TV camera, but this was over the top. I wondered why.

I explained that it was just a storm story and we put our car there for our own safety. He didn't buy it. Marty ignored the guy and kept shooting while I talked to (and distracted) the disgruntled man. Teamwork. We got enough video and left. I didn't find out why the guy was so angry until a couple of years later. Several firefighters had been indicted for shift trading—in short, a way for one firefighter to pay another firefighter to do his job for him; without even going to work, they kept insurance and other benefits. Turns out, he was one of them. All I can say is that he must have thought we were there to show he was home when he was supposed to be at work. I wish I had known; it would have been a great investigative story. I should have read more into his reaction!

The Damn Guy Made Me Choke Up

On my last day at WOIO, just before retirement, I was determined not to get emotional. I didn't, through many congratulations, and even a long interview they did with me for the news. I kept cool until they gave me a cake. I said thank you to everyone with no problem while acknowledging folks like Julia and others with whom I had worked closely every day. Then I got to Marty.

I told a joke that a former colleague of ours, Mike Olszewski, told some years earlier. "You probably didn't know it," he said, "But Marty DeChant has a candy bar named after him. It's called the Marty Bar. It's the only candy bar that tells you how good it is before you open it." I told the joke and got a laugh—and something hit me. I looked at Marty. "You are that good," I said, and my voice cracked.

EDDIE BELL

Eddie was a low-key guy. By the time I met him, he had seen it all, after probably thirty years of crisscrossing Ohio highways for Channel 3. No matter where we went, Eddie always knew a spot to eat where they made some ethnic specialty. Not just in Cleveland. We'd be coming up I-77, two or three hours south of Cleveland, and if time allowed, he'd say, "Orlo, there's a little spot over there just a few miles off the road that no one knows about. They have the best (fill in the blank) I've ever had. Let's eat there." We would walk in, and he was always greeted. They always remembered him. I reasoned that it was because of the way he had treated them in the past. A truly kind man. He was never wrong about the food, either. Sad that a lot of those hole-in-the-wall spots disappeared over the years, having been replaced by fast-food joints that are all alike.

Eddie was just a joy to work with. Always a positive attitude. A gem.

LARRY BAKER

From the first day I met Larry Baker, he predicted the death of television. Thirty-five or more years ago, when I first got to Channel 3, he told me, "You don't think this business is gonna be around long enough for you to retire, do you?" It was sobering, but I was young and thought he was full of crap. TV proved him wrong. Although it is not as strong as it used to be, it lasted long enough for me to comfortably retire. I tease him about his prediction to this day.

Each year we would prerecord a one-hour special at the Bernie Kosar Celebrity Golf Tournament. Bernie was from Youngstown, and he gave a lot back to the community. He had many of his quarterback friends and other celebs play in the tournament, which raised a lot of money for charity.

Larry and I were assigned to interview celebrity players. We scoped out a spot on the 16th hole the first year and used it every year after that. It was a par five, so usually there was a group on the green, one waiting to chip up, and one who had just teed off waiting for their second or third shot. Plenty of opportunities to get a quick soundbite without getting in the way of play.

The players were great. We talked to Jim Kelly from the Buffalo Bills, Ozzie Newsome, Hanford Dixon, many other Browns greats as well as other teams' QBs who were all Bernie's buddies. Even Meat Loaf, the "Bat Out of Hell" musician, had fun with us.

We only ever had one person be anything but gracious. One year, we went up to a former quarterback who was waiting to hit his second shot. I asked if we could talk to him. He said, "Yeah, make it quick." I thought it a bit brusque but asked a question. Larry said, "Hold on, I've got a problem." He put his camera to the ground and made an adjustment. It took a minute or so. At some point, the QB looked at Larry and said, "You gonna be OK?" Larry gave him a cold stare and said, "Yeah, I am." He picked up the camera, and before I could ask a question Larry said the camera still wasn't right. The camera was back on the ground and he continued to make changes in its settings. The QB looked down at him and almost in a mocking tone said, "I don't think you're gonna be OK." Larry's cold stare returned. "You seem to think that I care if you're on this special or not," Larry said. "And I don't care." The QB had no answer. He sat in the cart like a kid who had been scolded. Larry made his camera work; I asked a question or two, and we were done. And, by the way, it still wasn't time for the player to hit his second shot. We had wasted none of his time. It taught me a lesson. Larry set an example: Treat the stars like you treat everyone else when they are being unreasonable.

TOM LIVINGSTON

Last, but certainly not least, there is tall Tommy Livingston. I worked with Tom for three and a half years in the early 1980s at WEWS. We remain great friends. Tom is the guy who took one for the team in the encounter with Prince's bodyguard. We shared any number of helicopter adventures, airplane rides, and encounters with everyday folks. We slept in his van at Cape Kennedy, chased fires at Detroit's Devil's Night, and made a crazy tour of three states when the weather people said, "Don't leave your homes." Most importantly we have shared a lot of laughs. Another pro's pro in my eyes.

TV INVESTIGATIONS CHANGED

TOWARD THE END OF MY career in TV news, we seldom ran long, three- or even five-part investigations that used to be the staple of the ratings periods. Resources became scarce, and to be honest, most stations couldn't afford to keep a reporter off the air for a week or two to complete them. Turning stories every day became the rule. I and others had to change. Yet another reinvention of myself. I needed to have something with an edge to it every day. Luckily, after decades in Cleveland I had enough sources to survive yet another massive change in television.

THE NEWS "SOUP"

The news "soup," as I sometimes call it, is made from an ever-evolving recipe. A news department's philosophy, reporting style, and even its graphics are to a great extent controlled by the news director. But there is also great input from outside consultants. Too much, in my view. These are the people who tell every station, "Win with weather." In the meantime, as a reporter you are out on the street hearing people ask, "What's wrong with your station—don't they know it snows here in Cleveland?" All reporters hear it from the real people. Maybe the research was done in San Diego.

More important has been the glacial shift over the years inside any television station. In the past, the sales department wouldn't dare poke its nose in the news department. I once did a story about a certain brand of pickup truck that had engineering problems.

The story was true, but a big advertiser canceled tens of thousands of dollars in advertising. Not a word was said to me. Back then, the only bottom line was whether the story was true.

Over the years, that line of demarcation eroded, inch by inch. Sales had an increasing role in news content across the board. It was a frightening development to many, especially us reporters. Worse yet was the influence that the promotion departments had in shaping news content. I remember having a conversation with a station promotion person once, many years ago when I was a reporter dedicated solely to an investigative unit. I was telling him and the news director what my story was about. He kept cutting me off and suggesting that I include this or that element because it was more promotable. Elements that I didn't have and that weren't part of the investigation. I remember saying, "Here is how this works. My job is to do the stories: This is what I have and can prove. Your job is to promote what I have." The news director agreed, and that was the end of the meeting.

I have had news directors who were helpful, those who were a hinderance, and those who were just filling a chair. One of the problems in the television news business is that every time a news director is fired (and they usually are), you must prove yourself to the new one. Yes, you have a track record, but the new person doesn't know a lot about it. Also, being in a new job, the new boss doesn't want you to get the station sued because that would splash up on him or her. The result is that a lot of the freedoms you had to just go out and do your job had to be earned all over again.

This is not to point a finger at anyone in particular. This situation is common from small markets to big markets and has been for years now. Clearly it reaches to the networks as well. Fox News reporters and editors know the spin they are expected to take; CNN reporters and editors know the spin they are expected to take.

Another thing has changed. It used to be that you worked at four or five television stations before making it up to a market like Cleveland. Today you can get a job in a large market like Cleveland after a year or two in a small market.

Why? Advertising revenue isn't what it once was, due to viewership decline. Less revenue equals lower salaries and that equates to less-experienced reporters.

Those hired are eager to get here. Who wouldn't be? But these new hires in large part are younger than in the past, and being paid very low salaries compared to even thirty years ago. They are often renters, and so have little idea about the impact of a tax levy or other local issues that have long-term effects on the communities they live in.

The result of this change is a disservice to the public, I believe. But I am not a naïve guy; I know it is a reality that television station management must navigate today. And that's not an easy job, considering all the other sources for news that the audience has today—including many held right in the palm of a news consumer's hand.

I'm not being critical of the reporters. I was that guy in smaller markets at one time, so I get it. But this is Cleveland, where people here have heard the news from some of the best over the decades. The Cleveland audience deserves experienced reporters.

DIVERSITY CAME SLOWLY

When I grew up listening to radio and watching television, and when I started working in broadcasting, there were very few women on the air. And those were, for the most part, relegated to a role as the "women's editor."

By the time I got into television full time, that had begun to change. There were at least a few more women on the air and in management. When I was hired at WBNG in Binghamton, New York in 1976, the program director was Judy Girard. She was my supervisor on *The Morning Show*. Later she went on to great success with the networks. (Her roommate in college, Jessica Savitch, was another pioneer; she went on to break the glass ceiling and become a main news anchor on NBC.)

Another change was slower: Even into the early 1980s, newsrooms were largely dominated by white reporters (still mostly men). Few African American journalists were in prominent management or anchor positions. Over time that changed, but only gradually.

The news landscape eventually became more diverse, especially in recent years. I don't just mean Black and white. We now see more reporting from people with widely different backgrounds—Asian, Hispanic, Middle Eastern, and American Indian—who in the old days would have been passed over. They bring more perspectives to the news while reporting the facts. I think all Cleveland stations do a good job at this, but I must give props to my former employer WOIO and its current management for going to the extent and expense of launching a fully Hispanic daily news cast on its digital platforms, among other initiatives.

A television station should be a mirror of the community it serves. In the past, most were not. Today, more are. Sadly, some people may not like the change. I admire it and consider it essential for television to serve an ever-changing population and remain relevant.

MEDIA INFLUENCES

CERTAIN PEOPLE IN THE MEDIA influenced me during my career, and many of them also changed the way news is covered in Cleveland. Here are some of them . . .

ERIC BRAUN

At the beginning there was Eric Braun. He is the classic example of networking old-school style. He was a radio news guy in Cleveland who was the morning on-air foil for legendary DJ Don Imus at WGAR. When I met Eric, I was working with a former WGAR DJ, Bob Vernon, in Youngstown. He had made the switch to television. This was his first TV job. I was executive producer and we were trying to hire someone to be a weekend anchor. Eric sensed that radio news was dying and wanted to make a switch to TV, too. Bob and I tried to get him hired; but the GM wouldn't go for it.

Time went by and in Cleveland, Eric had a meteoric rise. First, he was hired as a reporter at WEWS TV, and very quickly became news director. In Youngstown, I was now the anchorman. Big problem, things went south in Youngstown, bad ratings and I had to leave. I called Eric and asked if he had anything open. He said all he had was a producer job. I said, "That is great. It is exactly what I want to do." Hell, I'd tell him anything to move up eighty-some spots in TV market size. Bob called Eric and gave me a good recommendation and Eric remembered that I had gone to bat for him on the weekend job in Youngstown. He hired me.

BOB VERNON

While working with Bob Vernon in Youngstown, I learned a lot. He was just learning television and I was his mentor in that regard. He had worked in big cities and I had not. He was my mentor on how to handle management. They wanted me to fill in and do the weather at some point. I was gonna say OK. Bob said, "That's fine, but before you do that ask them how much extra it pays." He was right. I did ask and got a few extra bucks every time I did it. He picked up TV quickly and had a successful career in Louisville and Raleigh.

RON BIELEK

Ron Bielek was a Cleveland native who had done a variety of jobs at WEWS and became a news director at various stations around the country. Channel 3 was lagging in the ratings and he was hired to come back to Cleveland to change the news culture at the station. He was way ahead of his time and underappreciated in some regards.

The station was owned and operated by NBC at the time. They had money to spend. They opened their wallets to lure me from WEWS. But before I arrived, there is a legendary story about Ron's arrival. NBC had a big welcoming party for him at a bar next door to the station. They introduced him, he was cheered, and he spoke. He shocked the crowd with his first sentence, "You all think you're pretty good, don't you? You make a lot of money, don't you? Well you suck and we're gonna change things and change a lot of you." Not the message they were expecting. He delivered on his promise. He shed many and hired me and others he liked from other stations.

One problem. He didn't get along with the general manager. Ron was basically hired by the network and not the GM. He always referred to the GM as "lard ass downstairs." We tried a lot of different things. He wanted an aggressive newscast, more like the one that I experienced years later at Channel 19 in 19 Action News. Management never let him go for it. 19 Action News was the brain-child of another TV genius, Bill Applegate.

BILL APPLEGATE

Applegate is legendary in the television business. He is the guy who fired Oprah Winfrey from her job in Chicago as a news anchor and decided she was better suited to be a talk-show host. That decision was as legendary as he was.

When he was coming to WOIO, I called a friend of mine, Paul Meincke, whom Applegate had hired in Chicago. I told him Applegate had been hired at my station. He said, "Hang on for the ride." He also mentioned that Bill's favorite book was *The Art of War*. Point taken. I read the book. Paul was right on. Bill instituted an aggressive, in-your-face style of news, 19 Action News. It was a rough ride for everyone, including me for a time. Many left the station. I survived. His format worked even though it took some time to get used to. At a Christmas party a year or so after he got here, he said to me, "I know we gave everyone a hard time. But it made you better. Now you are the poster child for the brand." Sur-viving in this business means adapting to many changing formats, styles, and personalities. I was reinvented once again. His next move was hiring Steve Doerr.

STEVE DOERR

Steve was another TV genius. He engineered some great stories and hired reporters and anchors who got a lot of attention. He also did what is most important to any TV station; he moved the needle. He got ratings. Steve is the guy who had a beautiful female reporter do a story while participating in a famous artist's all-nude "instal-lation." There were other controversial stories and hires. Bottom line, he raised ratings. Raising ratings means more advertising dollars and while news is a service, TV is also a business.

With the 19 Action News brand, I was always pushing the envelope. At least once or twice a month, I'd go into Steve's office after doing a story and say, "Did I go too far today?" His answer was always the same, "I'll let you know when you go too far." He never did!

DAN SALAMONE

Dan Salamone had a large influence on TV news in Cleveland in the 2000s. He was a quirky guy and came up with a quirky way to tell a story when cameras couldn't be used (see "The Puppet's Court" in the Court Stories chapter). He pretty much left me alone and never had a problem with what I did.

DAVID WITTMAN

David Wittman was hired as the main anchorman at WOIO when General Manager Bill Applegate was making massive changes and instituting the 19 Action News format. David is a rock-steady guy and will probably be surprised to find I've mentioned him. David had two major effects on me.

The first was one of his favorite sayings, "words mean things." His message was to choose them carefully. This was important as we turned to a far more aggressive style of news. He joked that his mother had been an English teacher and, in his words, "It is both a blessing and a curse." He was a nut on spelling, as well as the fact that choosing the right word can completely change the impact of a sentence or even a story. He urged everyone in the newsroom to use active verbs, never use the past tense. He was right. It conveyed "Action," which we were all about.

His second effect on me was that he knew how to carry himself as a professional. He was a guy who went to morning Mass every day except Saturday and carried the message with him. No loud outbursts, even when all hell was breaking loose. He was a steady force in what had become a far younger and less experienced newsroom than it had been. I know a lot of him rubbed off on me. I hope it showed in how I approached the job in the years after he retired.

LEON BIBB

And then there is Leon Bibb. What I write about Leon here is short but not intended to give short treatment to his effect on me. It is short because I have already written about the various effects that others have had on me. Each contributed something. This paragraph is short because if you could sum all of them up in one person, it is Leon Bibb. How to carry yourself, how to be aggressive while maintaining a journalistic integrity that is beyond reproach, how to use words to paint a picture, and so many more things that we saw in the years I have been fortunate enough to know him. Heck, we both even survived Ron Bielek. I make a joke, but there is no joke intended. He is one of the greatest men I have been fortunate enough to know and call a friend.

BOB TEAGUE

Over the years, I have often reflected on a book I read in the mid-1980s by Bob Teague, a reporter from WNBC in New York. He was one of the first Black journalists in the TV business. *Live and Off-Color: News Biz* was a great title. In the book, Teague was sharply critical of the commercialization of TV news, yet he kept working in it. Why? Something he said in reflecting on his own career has always stayed with me. It is a great reflection:

> So why did an old bird dog like me keep coloring his grey hairs and tackling every assignment as if it were the biggest story of the year? Personal pride was certainly a factor, along with the feeling that good work was my shield. Beyond that, out there in the field, I was still having fun chasing corpses, controversies, and catastrophes with a camera crew. What an

intoxicating ego trip. I was the screenwriter, director, narrator, and the star in hundreds of mini movies a year. I was amazed, amused, and adrenalized by the menagerie of personalities I encountered. I was also sex symbol with clout.

I used to keep the quote on my desk. His thoughts on getting up every day and doing what we all do as reporters are still a part of me. I don't know that the sex appeal part relates to me, but the rest of it is right on. It is the reason I got up every day hoping to uncover something and get another rush of news adrenaline.

STICK WITH YOUR ROOTS

I was raised by hard-working parents. They were the children of immigrants. The credo was, "Don't spend money you don't have, respect your elders, and you need a haircut." Typical baby boomer stuff. They weren't requests. They were expectations. I was often asked in newsrooms, "Orlo, who is your agent?" I never really had one. I venture to say that if my grandfather learned that I was giving a percentage of my wages to someone to represent me, I'd probably get cuffed in the back of the neck, with him saying something like, "What's wrong with you, you can't stand up for yourself?" That said, I have used lawyers, most notably Avery Friedman and Craig Brown, to review contract language and help me navigate contract negotiations. Avery has been a trusted friend and advisor to me for decades.

SUDDENLY, IT WAS OVER

THERE I WAS, ON JANUARY 31, 2020, standing in front of the assembled news team and others at television station WOIO. Next to news director Ian Rubin, the last of my twenty-one news directors over fifty years in the business. I had just cut a cake for my sendoff—my last day as a news reporter. Ian said a bunch of nice things, but likely the most accurate was when he said that I had been a pain in his neck. We all laughed, but I took great pride in that comment. That is what I always wanted to be: the guy questioning authority, asking questions, and getting to the truth.

What an unbelievable range of experiences I had had, reporting the news. Some of the many stories I recount in this book came to mind—and others, too. Like searching the State of Ohio's unclaimed funds website and finding $10,000 owed to an elderly woman in a poor neighborhood who was living on Social Security. Her heartfelt thank-you I will remember for life. Or using a radar gun to show parents that school buses loaded with kids were exceeding speed limits day after day. That time we camped outside a doctor's office and filmed proof that he was running a dangerous pill mill. Experiencing the eerie quiet amid the wreckage after a tornado has hit. Meeting sports stars, murderers, crime victims, panhandlers, judges . . . and thousands and thousands of regular folks.

I was so lucky to have had such a rich and varied career.

Now, I was done in the news business. I had begun thinking about it a few months earlier—maybe it was time to step aside. It had been my own choosing. But still, it was hard that day, realizing it really was over. Had I made a mistake? A flood of memories came to mind. It happened in a split-second. My wife, Kim, was there in the background as she always has been, supporting me at every turn for more than forty years. I have been through a lot; she has been through more in many ways. Most of it due to me, stories I have done, or enemies I made in a quest to get to the bottom of a story.

As I close, I'll steal a quote from the writings of legendary CBS newsman Mike Wallace. I'm not comparing myself to him—he's a giant, and I am just a guy who went to work every day at a job he loved, made a nice living, and tried to help people. I emphasize *tried* to help—it didn't always work. Wallace reflected on what he felt people thought of his on-air style: "You're egotistical, occasionally cruel and for many people, well-mannered people, the embodiment of everything they hate about reporters." He ended the thought by saying, "I've got to plead guilty, I suppose. You know, it comes with the territory."

It certainly came with the territory I covered. And I wouldn't change a thing.

I will end with the last words I ever said on television as a reporter. I was on set with anchor Tiffani Tucker, who did a beautiful farewell tribute piece on my retirement. I didn't remember saying the words live, but watching a video later, I saw that, at the end, I looked up, waved at the camera, and said, "Thank you." It was appropriate because I owe thanks to so many people who helped me along the way. As I watched the video, it hit me and bears repeating, I really am the luckiest guy in the world.

Thank you!

HOW DO YOU SAY THANK YOU?

MY WIFE, KIM, HAS PUT up with a lot from me, in many ways. We met in 1976, when I made $150 a week. We were engaged a few months later and married only about fifteen months after meeting. She was twenty-one when we got married and I was twenty-four. All of the stories I tell in this book (and many more)—particularly the troubling ones—she has suffered through from a distance. She maintained a calm setting for our family at home despite the worry, my long hours at work, and, yes, the threats.

Some of the threats were indeed serious. Others were kind of funny. One day, Kim came home from the market and told me that two women were talking about a story I had reported about a local official in our town. They saw her and stopped talking. When she passed by and turned to go down another aisle, she heard one say with scorn, "That's his wife."

Kim has also endured my repeating many of the stories I've written about here for more than forty years. She was already tired of hearing them when she had to endure them yet again while she edited the manuscript for this book (because of my lousy grammar!).

I love Kim for pushing through the troubling situations—usually ones I caused by putting my job first. She has had to ask schools to keep an eye on our child due to threats, and she has had to ask our town's police department to watch the house on a few occasions. Where was I? At work!

Once when accepting an award I came close to properly expressing my gratitude for all Kim has done for me. "You really only have to make one important decision in your life," I said. "You have to marry the right person. And I did." Close, but no cigar.

So here I will share something I have never shared. One thing that only Kim knows. In my whole life, I have only said the words "I love you," romantically, to one person, and that is Kim.

OTHER BOOKS OF INTEREST . . .

Cleveland Cops
The Real Stories They Tell Each Other

John H. Tidyman

Gritty, hilarious, and heartbreaking, these remarkable true stories take you on the roller coaster ride that is life as a Cleveland police officer. Listen in on stories the rest of us rarely get to hear: The biggest arrests, dumbest criminals, funniest practical jokes, and scariest moments. It's an inside look at the toughest job in town.

"This book should be required reading for every elected official and for every citizen." – Chief Edward P. Kovacic (retired), Cleveland Police Department

Cleveland TV Tales
Stories from the Golden Age of Local Television

Mike & Janice Olszewski

Remember when TV was just three channels and the biggest celebrities in Cleveland were a movie host named Ghoulardi, an elf named Barnaby, and a newscaster named Dorothy Fuldheim? Revisit the early days in these lively stories about the pioneering entertainers who invented television programming before our very eyes. Filled with fun details.

The Buzzard
Inside the Glory Days of WMMS and Cleveland Rock Radio—A Memoir

John Gorman, Tom Feran

This rock and roll radio memoir goes behind the scenes at the nation's hottest station during FM's heyday, from 1973 to 1986. It was a wild and creative time. John Gorman and a small band of true believers remade rock radio while Cleveland staked its claim as the "Rock and Roll Capital." Filled with juicy insider details.

"John Gorman describes in exclusive, behind-the-scenes detail the state of rock 'n' roll from the early '70s to the late '80s, when just about anything happened and everyone looked the other way . . . This is essential reading for musicians, entertainment industry leaders, and music fans alike." – Mike Shea, CEO/Co-Founder, Alternative Press magazine

More at **www.grayco.com**

OTHER BOOKS OF INTEREST . . .

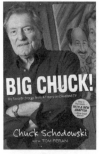

Big Chuck!
My Favorite Stories from 47 Years on Cleveland TV

Chuck Schodowski, Tom Feran

A beloved Cleveland TV legend tells funny and surprising stories from a lifetime in television. "Big Chuck" collaborated with Ernie Anderson on the groundbreaking "Ghoulardi" show and continued to host a late-night show across four decades—the longest such run in TV history. Packed with behind-the-scenes details about TV and celebrities.

"A vivid picture of an honest man in the insane world of television. Highly recommended." – Midwest Book Review

Smoky, Sweaty, Rowdy, and Loud
Tales of Cleveland's Legendary Rock & Roll Landmarks

Mike & Janice Olszewski

These stories go backstage at legendary Cleveland rock music venues of the 1950s to '90s—clubs like the Agora and the Phantasy; halls like Public Auditorium and the Cleveland Arena; bars like the Euclid Tavern and Leo's Casino; haunts like Swingo's; the cavernous Municipal Stadium—and more. Told by and about the people who worked and rocked there.

Cleveland Radio Tales
Stories from the Local Radio Scene of the 1960s, '70s, '80s, and '90s

Mike & Janice Olszewski

Remember when Cleveland radio crackled with larger-than-life characters? Meet dozens of intriguing personalities like "Count" John Manolesco, the talk show host and former vampire who performed an exorcism live on-air, a daytime jock who once did his show in the nude, teenage "pirate" radio operators, unruly studio guests, and many more true tales.

More at **www.grayco.com**